Acknowledgments and credits appear on pages 438–439, which constitutes an extension of this copyright page.

Copyright © 2000 by Scholastic Inc.   All rights reserved.   Printed in the U.S.A.

ISBN 0-439-06149-0

SCHOLASTIC, SCHOLASTIC LITERACY PLACE, and associated logos and designs are trademarks and/or registered trademarks of Scholastic Inc.

4 5 6 7 8 9 10   09   07 06 05 04 03 02 01 00

TABLE OF CONTENTS

STORY STUDIO

THEME
People express themselves through stories and pictures.

FAIRY TALE

The Gingerbread Man...... **12**
retold by Jim Aylesworth
illustrated by Barbara McClintock

MAP
Tricksters from
Around the World **41**
from *Storyworks*

FOLK TALE VARIANT

**Abuelo and
The Three Bears** **44**
by Jerry Tello
illustrated by Ana López Escrivá

POEM
Who's Been Sleeping
in My Porridge? **59**
by Colin McNaughton
from *Big Bear's Treasury*

FANTASY

**Little Grunt
and the Big Egg**........... **62**
by Tomie dePaola

MENTOR **88**
Author and Artist **Tomie dePaola**

ENGLISH FOLK TALE

Red Riding Hood **94**
retold and illustrated
by James Marshall

FOLK TALES
And Still More Tales **118**

REALISTIC FICTION

Amazing Grace **122**
by Mary Hoffman
illustrated by Caroline Binch

THEATER PROGRAM
An Amazing Peter Pan **142**

GLOSSARY **426**

UNIT 4

TABLE OF CONTENTS

Animal World

THEME
We use information
to understand
the interdependence
of people and animals.

FANTASY

Stellaluna **150**
by Janell Cannon

NONFICTION

**Balto: The Dog
Who Saved Nome** **194**
by Margaret Davidson
illustrated by Cathie Bleck

MAGAZINE

Puppygarten Star **210**
photographed by Justin Sutcliffe
from *KidCity Magazine*

NONFICTION

**Ibis: A True
Whale Story** **214**
by John Himmelman

PHOTO ESSAY

Working With Whales **232**

REALISTIC FICTION

**When the Monkeys
Came Back** **236**
by Kristine L. Franklin
illustrated by Robert Roth

MENTOR **258**
Zoo Curator **Lisa Stevens**

FINE ARTS

from **How Artists
See Animals** **264**
by Colleen Carroll

FINE ARTS

Animal Messengers **276**
from *Colorín Colorado:
The Art of Indian Children*

GLOSSARY **426**

ALASKA

NOME
SAFETY

ANCHORAGE

N
W E
S

UNIT 5

TABLE OF CONTENTS

LEND A HAND

THEME

People can make a difference in their communities.

REALISTIC FICTION

The Little Painter of Sabana Grande **284**
by Patricia Maloney Markun
illustrated by Robert Casilla

PHOTO ESSAY

from My Painted House, My Friendly Chicken, and Me **308**
by Maya Angelou
photographed by
Margaret Courtney-Clarke

NONFICTION

Fire Fighters. 316
by Robert Maass

MENTOR. 340
Police Officer **Nadine Jojola**

BIOGRAPHY

from **The Many Lives
of Benjamin Franklin**. 346
by Aliki

SONG
Yankee Doodle. 356

HISTORICAL FICTION

**Follow the
Drinking Gourd** 362
by Jeanette Winter

ARTICLE
The Underground
Railroad. 390
by Glennette Turner
illustrated by Jerry Pinkney

POEM

Miss Spider's Tea Party . . 394
by David Kirk

GLOSSARY. 426

UNIT 6

STORY STUDIO

THEME

People express themselves through stories and pictures.

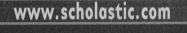

The Gingerbread Man **12**
retold by Jim Aylesworth

Tricksters from Around the World **41**

Abuelo and The Three Bears **44**
by Jerry Tello

Who's Been Sleeping in My Porridge? **59**
by Colin McNaughton

Little Grunt and the Big Egg **62**
by Tomie dePaola

MENTOR
Author and Artist **Tomie dePaola** **88**

Red Riding Hood **94**
retold and illustrated by James Marshall

And Still More Tales **118**

Amazing Grace **122**
by Mary Hoffman

An Amazing Peter Pan **142**

GLOSSARY **426**

UNIT 4

Welcome to

LITERACY PLACE

Visit an Author's Studio

People express themselves through stories and pictures.

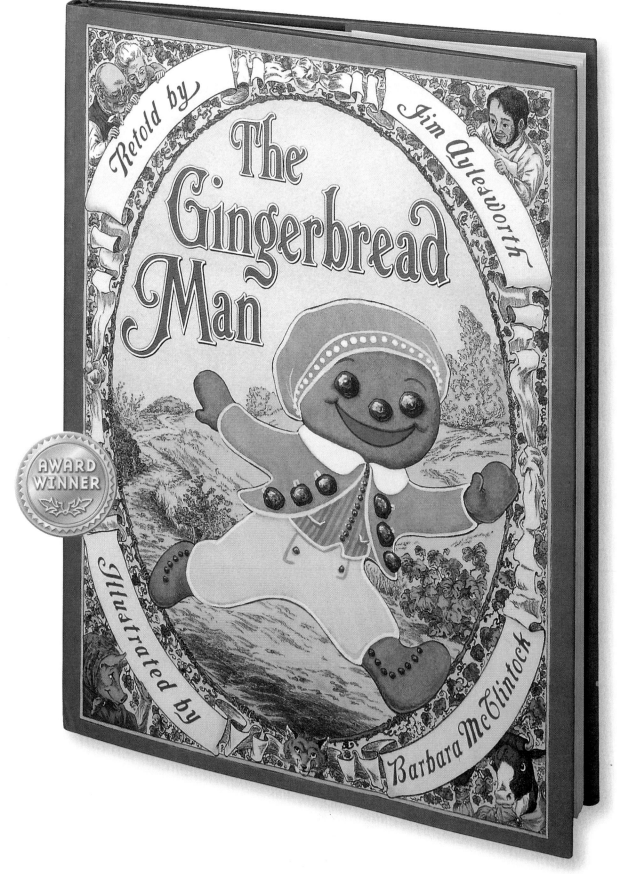

Once upon a time,
there was a little old man and a little old woman.

One day, the little old woman said, "Let's make a gingerbread man!"

"Yes, let's do!" said the little old man, and they did.

So, they mixed up the batter,

and they rolled out the dough,

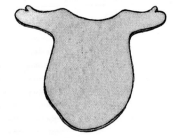

and they shaped
the little arms,

and they shaped
the little legs,

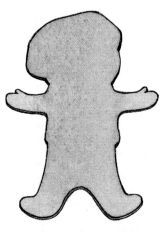

and they shaped
the little head.

And with raisins, they made the little eyes and the little nose and the little mouth, and then with sugar glaze, they dressed him in a fancy suit of clothes.

When all was set, they put the gingerbread man into the oven, and they waited.

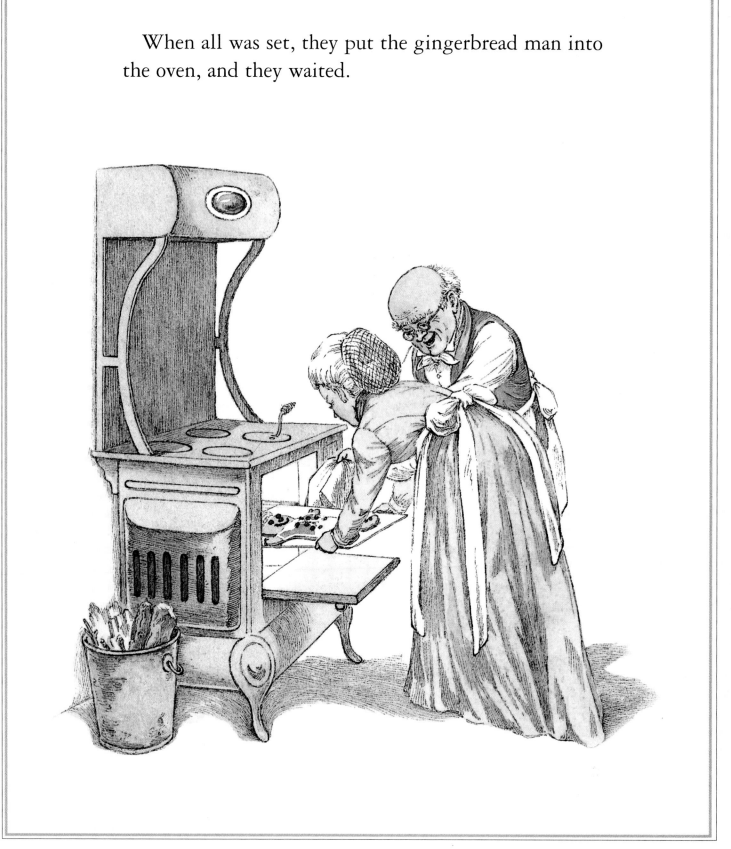

Pretty soon, a delicious smell coming from the oven told them that the gingerbread man was ready, and so were they!

18

But when they opened the oven door, out popped
the Gingerbread Man, and he ran across the floor.

The little old man and the little old woman could hardly believe their eyes! The Gingerbread Man looked up at them, put his little hands on his hips, and said,

"Run! Run!
Fast as you can!
You can't catch me!
I'm the Gingerbread Man!"

The little old man reached down to grab him, but quick as a wink, the Gingerbread Man ran out the door and down the road, and the little old man and the little old woman ran after him.

"Come back! Come back!" they yelled. But the Gingerbread Man just looked over his shoulder, and said,

"No! No!
I won't come back!
I'd rather run
Than be your snack!"

And he kept on running.

And he ran,

and he ran,

and he ran,

and after a time, he met a butcher standing in front of his shop. The Gingerbread Man looked up at him, put his little hands on his hips, and said,

"Run! Run!
Fast as you can!
You can't catch me!
I'm the Gingerbread Man!
I've run from a husband!
I've run from a wife!
And I'll run from you, too!
I can! I can!"

The butcher reached down to grab him, but quick as a wink, the Gingerbread Man ran on down the road, and the butcher ran after him!

"**Come back!**" yelled the butcher.

And not far behind, the little old man and the little old woman were yelling, too! "**Come back! Come back!**"

But the Gingerbread Man just looked over his shoulder, and said,

"No! No!
I won't come back!
I'd rather run
Than be your snack!"

And he kept on running! And he ran, and he ran, and he ran.

And after a time he met a black-and-white cow. The Gingerbread Man looked up at her, put his little hands on his hips, and said,

"Run! Run!
Fast as you can!
You can't catch me!
I'm the Gingerbread Man!
I've run from a husband!
I've run from a wife!
I've run from a butcher
With a carving knife!
And I'll run from you, too!
I can! I can!"

The black-and-white cow reached out to grab him. But quick as a wink, the Gingerbread Man ran on down the road, and the black-and-white cow ran after him!

"Come back!" yelled the black-and-white cow.
And not far behind, the little old man, and the little old woman, and the butcher with the knife were yelling, too!

"Come back! Come back! Come back!"

But the Gingerbread Man just looked over his shoulder, and said,

"No! No!
I won't come back!
I'd rather run
Than be your snack!"

And he kept on running. And he ran, and he ran, and he ran.

And after a time, he met a muddy old sow.

The Gingerbread Man looked up at her, put his little hands on his hips, and said,

"Run! Run!
Fast as you can!
You can't catch me!
I'm the Gingerbread Man!
I've run from a husband!
I've run from a wife!
I've run from a butcher
With a carving knife!
I've run from a cow
All black and white!
And I'll run from you, too!
I can! I can!"

The muddy old sow reached out to grab him. But quick as a wink, the Gingerbread Man ran on down the road, and the muddy old sow ran after him!

"Come back!" yelled the muddy old sow.

And not far behind, the little old man, and the little old woman, and the butcher with the knife, and the black-and-white cow were yelling, too!

"Come back! Come back! Come back! Come back!"

But the Gingerbread Man just looked over his shoulder, and said,

"No! No!
I won't come back!
I'd rather run
Than be your snack!"

And he kept on running.

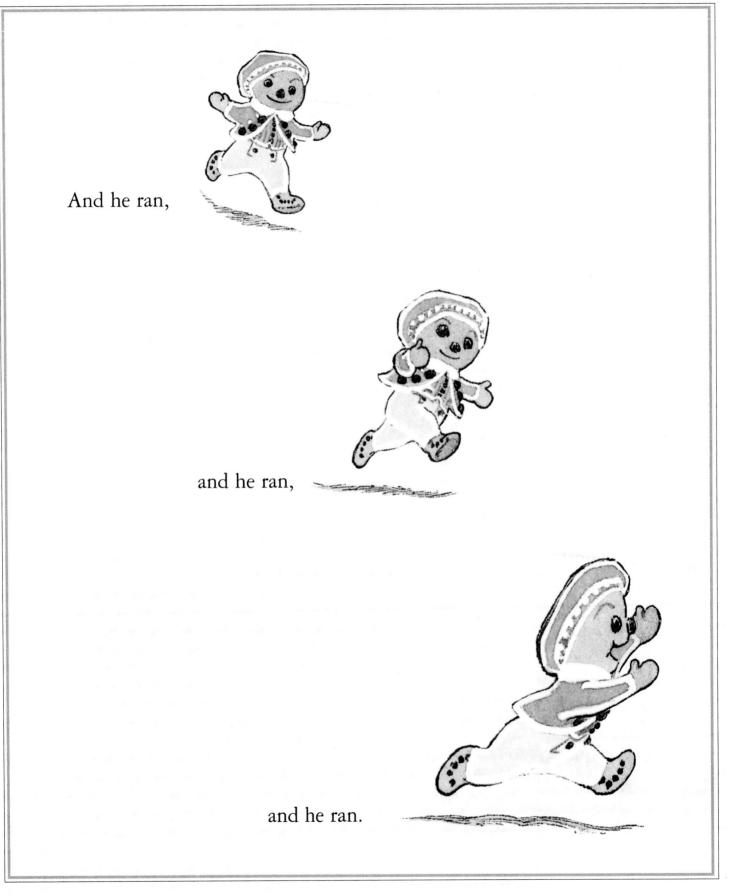

And he ran,

and he ran,

and he ran.

And after a time, he met a fox. The
Gingerbread Man looked at him, put his
little hands on his hips, and said,

"Run! Run!
Fast as you can!
You can't catch me!
I'm the Gingerbread Man!
I've run from a husband!
I've run from a wife!
I've run from a butcher
With a carving knife!
I've run from a cow,
And a muddy old sow,
And I'll run from you, too!
I can! I can!"

33

"What did you say?" asked the fox. The tricky fox pretended that he couldn't hear well. "I'm not as young as I used to be," he said. "You'll have to come closer and speak louder."

The Gingerbread Man stepped closer, and in a very loud voice, he said,

"Run! Run!
Fast as you can!
You can't catch me!
I'm the Gingerbread Man!
I've run from a husband!
I've run from a wife!
I've run from a butcher
With a carving knife!
I've run from a cow,
And a muddy old sow,
And I'll run from you, too!
I can! I can!"

Just then, the little old man, and the little old woman, and the butcher with the knife, and the black-and-white cow, and the muddy old sow came running around a turn in the road! And they were yelling!
"Come back! Come back! Come back! Come back!"

The Gingerbread Man looked over
his shoulder, but before he could say
a single word, the fox jumped up and
grabbed him!

And quick as a wink,
Before he could think,
With a snap and a snick,
And a lap and a lick,
The Gingerbread Man
Was gone!

The little old man, and the little old woman, and the butcher with his knife, and the black-and-white cow, and the muddy old sow all stood and stared sadly at the fox. He hadn't left a single crumb for anyone.

Riddle-riddle ran, fiddle-fiddle fan,
So ends the tale of the Gingerbread Man.

Folk Tale Map

Tricksters

From Around the World

Did you know that trickster tales are popular around the world? All trickster characters are animals. They all have human qualities, and use their brains to outwit stronger animals. But different cultures have their own favorite tricksters. Here are four clever tricksters.

COYOTE
Native American
A favorite character among Native Americans from the Great Plains, Coyote can morph into the form of any creature.

FOX
European
The greedy fox appears in many European tales.

PARROT
Central and South American
Papagayo the noisy parrot uses his cunning to outwit the wicked moon-dog.

SPIDER
West African
The spider named Anansi has special powers. Anansi is also popular in the Caribbean.

Think About Reading

Think about *The Gingerbread Man*. Finish each sentence in the story map. Do your work on another sheet of paper. Draw pictures to go with your sentences.

Character

1. First the Gingerbread Man ran away from _____ and _____ .

Problem

2. Next the Gingerbread Man ran away from _____ .

3. Next the Gingerbread Man ran away from _____ .

4. Next the Gingerbread Man ran away from _____ .

Ending

5. At last the fox _____ .

Write a New Ending

The fox eats the Gingerbread Man at the end of the story. Continue the story. What do you think might happen next? Add a page to tell about it. Write what might happen and draw a picture to go with what you write.

Literature Circle

Which of the tricksters is a character in *The Gingerbread Man*? What might some of the other tricksters do if they met the Gingerbread Man?

Author
Jim Aylesworth

Jim Aylesworth likes to keep in touch with the children who read his stories. Aylesworth visits schools so he can meet and talk with his readers. He has his own homepage on the Internet, where he lists his address and his e-mail address. Aylesworth says, "I love hearing from my fans, and I try to answer all the letters I receive."

More Books by
Jim Aylesworth

- *Through the Night*
- *My Sister's Rusty Bike*
- *McGraw's Emporium*

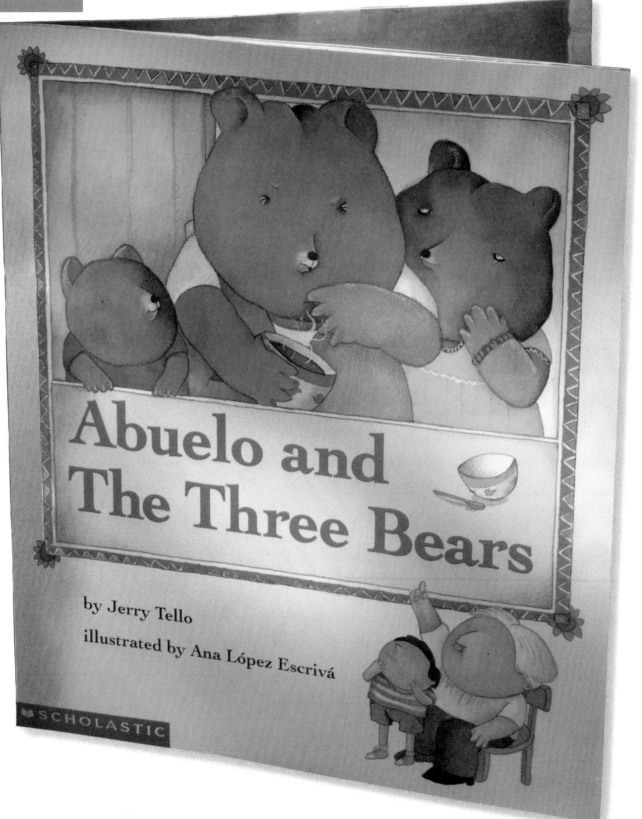

Abuelo and The Three Bears

by Jerry Tello

illustrated by Ana López Escrivá

SCHOLASTIC

It was a quiet Sunday. Emilio and his grandfather sat on the front porch.

"Abuelo," said Emilio, "do we have to wait much longer? When will everybody get here?"

"Your cousins will arrive soon," Abuelo answered, "and we'll have a fine dinner. I'll tell you a story to help pass the time."

Once there were three bears who lived in the woods—
Papá Bear, Mamá Bear, and their little Osito. One Sunday
morning, Papá Bear woke up as grumpy as ever. Then he
smelled something good. "Mmmm, frijoles!" he said.

"Abuelo, you're joking!" laughed Emilio.
"Bears don't like beans!"
"Well, all the bears I know like frijoles,"
said Abuelo.

46

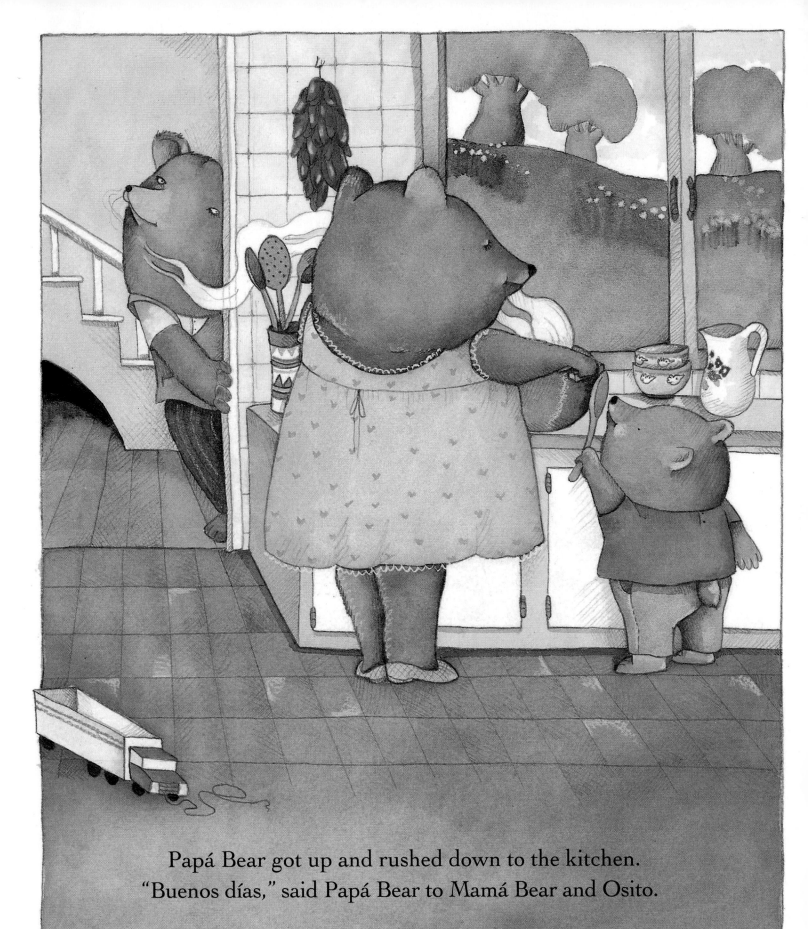

Papá Bear got up and rushed down to the kitchen.
"Buenos días," said Papá Bear to Mamá Bear and Osito.

Papá Bear sat down at the table and tucked a napkin under his chin. "How are the frijoles? Are they ready yet?" he asked.

"Yes," answered Mamá Bear, "but they're still too hot to eat."

"I can't wait," said Papá Bear. "I'm so hungry I could eat an elephant."

"Abuelo," said Emilio, "bears don't eat elephants."

"Emilio," answered Abuelo, "you must never argue with a hungry bear."

Stubborn Papá Bear didn't listen to Mamá Bear's warning.

"¡Ay!" he growled, jumping out of his chair. "These beans are too hot!"

"I told you so," said Mamá Bear. "Why don't we take a walk into town while they cool?"

"All right," grumbled Papá Bear, whose mouth was still burning. So the bears left their breakfast to cool and went out.

Just then, in another part of the woods, a girl named Trencitas set out from her house to visit her friend, Osito. She was called Trencitas because she had long black braids.

"Abuelo," Emilio called out, "the girl in this story is called Goldilocks and she has blond hair."

"Goldilocks?" Abuelo shrugged. "In my story it was Trencitas with her long black braids who came to visit. And she was hungry, too!"

When Trencitas arrived at Osito's house, she noticed
that the door was open. So she stepped inside and followed
her nose until she came to the three bowls of beans.

First Trencitas tasted some beans
from the great big bowl, but they
were too hot. Then she tasted some
from the medium-sized bowl, but
they were too cold. Finally she
tasted some from the little bowl, and
they were just right. So she finished
them all up.

Now Trencitas decided to sit in the
living room and wait for the bears to
return. She sat in the great big chair,
but it was too hard. She sat in the
medium-sized chair, but it was too soft.
Then she sat in the little chair, and it
was just right until. . . CRASH!

"Abuelo, what's Trencitas going to do?" asked Emilio. "She broke her friend's chair."

"Don't worry," Abuelo said. "She'll come back later with glue and leave it like new."

Trencitas was feeling very sleepy. She went upstairs to take a rest. First she tried the great big bed, but the blanket was scratchy. Then she tried the medium-sized bed, but it was too lumpy. Finally she tried the little bed. It was too small, but it was so cozy and soft that Trencitas soon fell asleep.

When the three bears came home, Papá Bear headed straight to the kitchen to eat his frijoles.

"¡Ay!" he growled when he saw his bowl. "Somebody's been eating my beans."

"And somebody's been eating my beans," said Mamá Bear.

"And there's only one bean left in my bowl," said Osito.

Then the three bears went into the living room.

"¡Ay!" said Papá Bear, when he saw that his chair had been moved. "Somebody's been sitting in my chair."

"And somebody's been sitting in my chair," said Mamá Bear.

"And my chair is all over the place!" said Osito.

The three bears climbed the stairs to check out the
bedrooms. Papá Bear went first. Mamá Bear and Osito
followed behind him.

"¡Ay!" said Papá Bear, when he looked in the bedroom.
"Somebody's been sleeping in my bed."

"And somebody's been sleeping in my bed," said Mamá Bear.

"Look who's sleeping in my bed!" said Osito. He ran over to Trencitas and woke her up. Then they all had a good laugh.

By now it was getting late. Mamá Bear said they'd walk Trencitas home to make sure she got there safely.

Papá Bear did not like this idea. "Another walk!" he growled. "What about my frijoles?"

"There'll be beans at my house," offered Trencitas.

"I'll bet that made Papá Bear happy," said Emilio.

"You're right," said Abuelo. "Here's what happened next . . . ."

55

When they all arrived at Trencitas's house, they sat down at a long table with Trencitas's parents, grandparents, uncles, aunts, and lots of cousins. They ate pork and fish and chicken and tortillas and beans and salsa so hot it brought tears to their eyes. And they laughed and shared stories.

"So you see, Emilio," said Abuelo, "Papá Bear had to wait a long time to eat his frijoles. But, in the end, he had a wonderful meal and lots of fun, just as you will when your cousins arrive."

"Is that the end of the story?"
Emilio asked.

"Yes," answered Abuelo, "and
it's the end of your waiting, too!"

GLOSSARY

Abuelo	Grandfather
Osito	Little Bear
Frijoles	Beans
Buenos días	Good morning
¡Ay!	Oh!
Trencitas	Little Braids
Tortillas	Thin corn pancakes
Salsa	Spicy tomato and chile dip

WHO'S BEEN SLEEPING IN MY PORRIDGE?

by Colin McNaughton

"Who's been sitting in my bed?"
   said the mama bear crossly.
"Who's been eating my chair?"
   said the baby bear weepily.
"Who's been sleeping in my porridge?"
   said the papa bear angrily.
"Wait a minute," said Goldilocks.

"Why can't you guys just stick
   to the script? Now let's try it
again and this time, no messing around."

Think About Reading

1. Who tells Emilio the story about the three bears?

2. Why isn't the girl who visits the bears called Goldilocks?

3. How do you think Osito feels when he finds Trencitas in his bed?

4. *Abuelo and The Three Bears* tells two stories. Which of these stories could really happen?

5. How is *Abuelo and The Three Bears* like "Who's Been Sleeping in My Porridge"?

Write Cartoon Dialogue

What if Trencitas and Goldilocks met? What do you think they would say to each other? Draw a cartoon of the two story characters. Draw speech balloons in your cartoon. In each character's balloon, write the words she would say.

Literature Circle

Talk about the pictures in *Abuelo and The Three Bears* and "Who's Been Sleeping in My Porridge?" How do the pictures help you understand the story and the poem? How do they help make the story and the poem funny? Which pictures do you like better? Why?

Author
Jerry Tello

When Jerry Tello was a teenager, he was often asked to baby-sit for his younger brothers and sisters. He soon found that telling them funny stories was a good way to keep them happy. Tello still makes children happy by telling stories. Now he travels all over the country, telling stories in both Spanish and English.

More Books by Jerry Tello
- *Coyote: How He Gets His Name*
- *Amalia and the Grasshopper*
- *A New Batch of Tortillas*

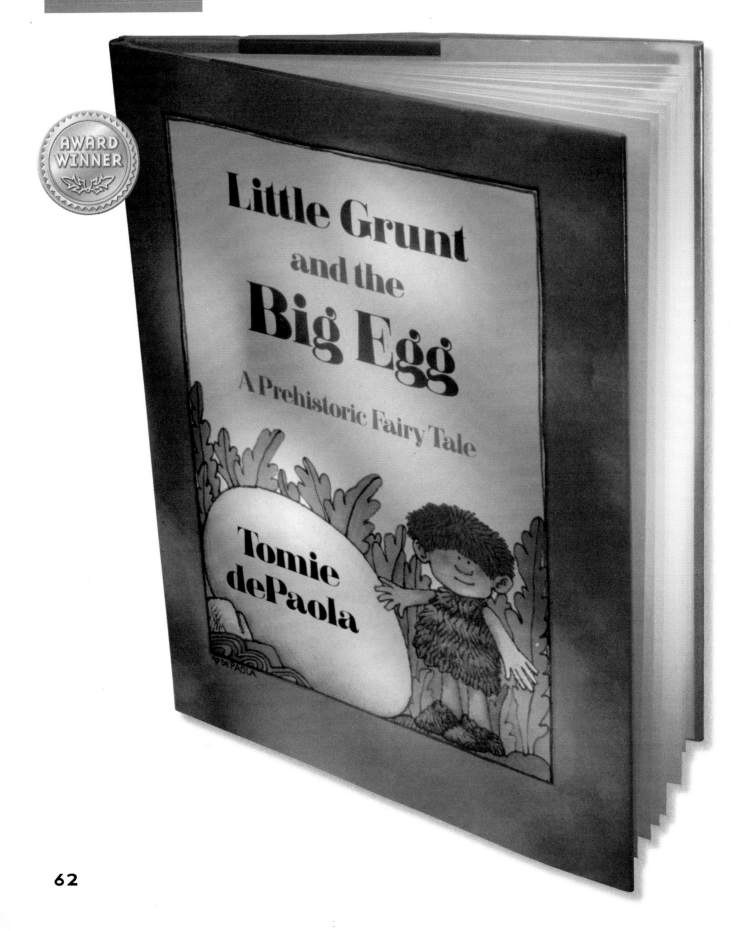

AWARD WINNER

Little Grunt
and the
Big Egg

A Prehistoric Fairy Tale

Tomie dePaola

Once upon a time, in a big cave, past the volcano on the left, lived the Grunt Tribe. There was Unca Grunt, Ant Grunt, Granny Grunt, Mama Grunt, and Papa Grunt. Their leader was Chief Rockhead Grunt. The smallest Grunt of all was Little Grunt.

One Saturday morning, Mama Grunt said to Little Grunt, "Little Grunt, tomorrow the Ugga-Wugga Tribe is coming for Sunday brunch. Could you please go outside and gather two dozen eggs?"

"Yes, Mama Grunt," said Little Grunt, and off he went.

At that time of year, eggs were hard to find. Little Grunt looked and looked. No luck. He was getting tired.

"What am I going to do?" he said to himself. "I can't find a single egg. I'll try one more place."

And it was a good thing that he did, because there, in the one more place, was the biggest egg Little Grunt had ever seen.

It was too big to carry. It was too far to roll. And besides, Little Grunt had to be very careful. Eggs break *very* easily.

Little Grunt thought and thought.

"I know," he said. He gathered some of the thick pointy leaves that were growing nearby. He wove them into a mat. Then he carefully rolled the egg on top of it. He pulled and pulled and pulled the egg all the way home.

"My goodness," said the Grunt Tribe. "Ooga, ooga, what an egg! That will feed us *and* the Ugga-Wuggas. And even the Grizzler Tribe. Maybe we should invite *them* to Sunday brunch, too."

"I'll be able to make that special omelet I've been wanting to," said Mama Grunt.

"Ooga, ooga! Yummy! Yummy!" said all the Grunts.

They put the egg near the hearth, and then they all went to bed.

That night, by the flickering firelight, the egg began to make noise. CLICK, CRACK went the egg. CLICK, CRACK, CLUNK. A big piece fell to the floor. CLICK, CRACK, CLUNK, PLOP. The egg broke in half, and instead of the big egg sitting by the fire . . .

There was a baby dinosaur!

"Waaangh," cried the baby dinosaur. And all the Grunt
Tribe woke up.

"Ooga, ooga!" they said. "What are we going to do?"

"There goes the brunch!" said Unca Grunt.

"What will the Ugga-Wuggas say?" said Ant Grunt.

"I bet I'm allergic to that thing," said Papa Grunt.

Chief Rockhead Grunt said, "All I know is it can't stay . . ."

But before he could finish, Little Grunt said, "May I keep him? Please? *Please*?"

"Every boy needs a pet," said Granny Grunt.

Some of the Grunts said yes. Some of the Grunts said no. But it was finally decided that Little Grunt could keep the baby dinosaur.

"Against my better judgment," mumbled Chief Rockhead Grunt.

"Oh, well, I suppose I can make pancakes for Sunday brunch," said Mama Grunt.

"I'm going to call him George," said Little Grunt.

Little Grunt and George became great pals.

But there was a problem. The cave stayed the same size, but George didn't. He began to grow.

And GROW. And GROW.

The cave got very crowded.

And there were other problems.

George wasn't housebroken.

George ate ALL the leaves off ALL the trees and ALL the bushes ALL around the cave. But still he was hungry.

George liked to play—rough. George stepped on things.

And when he sneezed—well, it was a disaster.

"Ooga, ooga! Enough is enough!" said the Grunts.

"Either that dinosaur goes, or I go," said Unca Grunt.

"I spend all day getting food for him," said Ant Grunt.

"Achoo!" said Papa Grunt. "I told you I was allergic to him."

"He stepped on all my cooking pots and broke them," said Mama Grunt.

"I guess it wasn't a good idea to keep him," said
Granny Grunt. "How about a nice *little* cockroach.
They make nice pets."

"I'm in charge here," said Chief Rockhead Grunt.
"And I say, *That giant lizard goes!*"

"Ooga, ooga! Yes! Yes!" said all the Grunts.

"But you promised," said Little Grunt.

The next morning, Little Grunt took George away
from the cave, out to where he had found him in the
first place.

"Good-bye, George," said Little Grunt. "I'll sure
miss you."

"Waaargh," said George.

Big tears rolled down both their cheeks. Sadly, Little Grunt watched as George walked slowly into the swamp.

"I'll never see him again," sobbed Little Grunt.

The days and months went by, and Little Grunt still missed George. He dreamed about him at night and drew pictures of him by day.

"Little Grunt certainly misses that dinosaur," said Mama Grunt.

"He'll get over it," said Papa Grunt.

"It's nice and peaceful here again," said Ant and Unca Grunt.

"I still say a cockroach makes a nice pet," said Granny Grunt.

"Ooga, ooga. Torches out. Everyone in bed," said Chief Rockhead.

That night, the cave started to shake. The floor
began to pitch, and loud rumblings filled the air.
  "Earthquake!" cried the Grunts, and they rushed
to the opening of the cave.

"No, it's not," said Granny Grunt. "Look! Volcano!"

And sure enough, the big volcano was erupting all over the place. Steam and rocks and black smoke shot out of the top. Around the cave, big rocks and boulders tumbled and bounced.

"We're trapped! We're trapped!" shouted the Grunts. "What are we going to do?"

"Don't ask me!" said Chief Rockhead. "I resign."

"Now we have no leader," cried Ant Grunt.

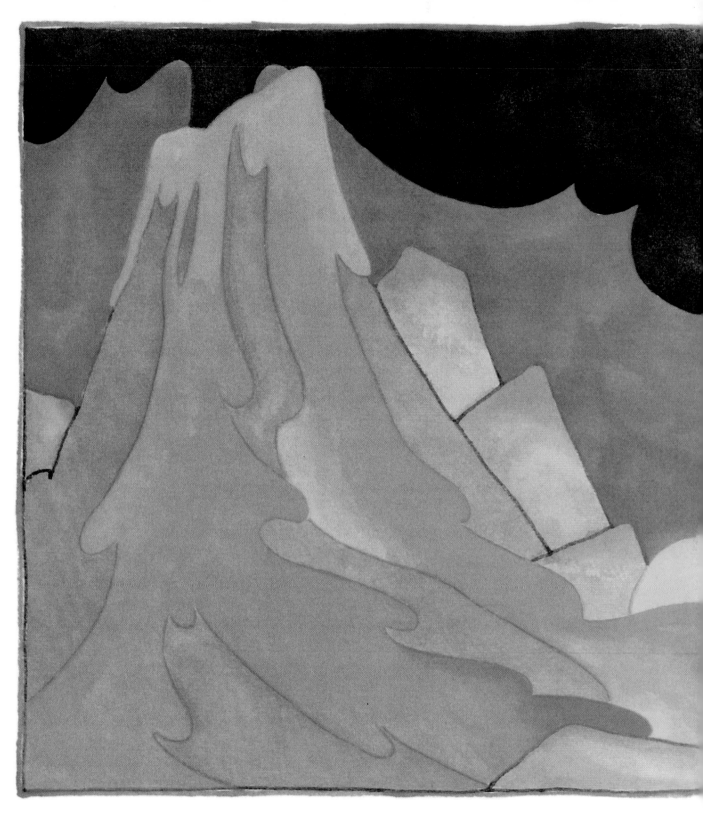

"Now we're really in trouble!" shouted Papa Grunt.
The lava was pouring out of the volcano in a wide,
flaming river and was heading straight for the cave.

There wasn't enough time for the Grunts to escape.

All of a sudden, the Grunts heard a different noise.

"Waaargh! Wonk!"

"It's George," cried Little Grunt. "He's come to save us."

"Ooga, ooga! Quick!" said the Grunts as they all jumped on George's long neck and long back and long tail.

And before you could say Tyrannosaurus rex,
George carried them far away to safety.

"As your new leader," Papa Grunt said, "I say this is our new cave!"

"I like the kitchen," said Mama Grunt.

"Now, when I was the leader . . ." said Plain Rockhead Grunt.

"When do we eat?" said Unca Grunt.

"I can't wait to start decorating," said Ant Grunt.

"I always say a change of scenery keeps you from getting old," said Granny Grunt.

"And George can live right next door," said
Little Grunt.

"Where is George?" asked Mama Grunt. "I haven't
seen him all afternoon."

"Ooga, ooga. Here, George," called the Grunts.

"Waaargh," answered George.

"Look!" said Little Grunt.

"Oh no!" said the Grunts.

There was George, sitting on a pile of big eggs.

"I guess I'd better call George Georgina!"
said Little Grunt.
And they all lived happily ever after.

MENTOR

Tomie dePaola

Author and Artist

An author can make ANYTHING happen in a story. And so can YOU!

Do you like to draw pictures? When Tomie dePaola was a little boy, he loved drawing so much that he decided to become an artist. He dreamed of telling stories someday with his art.

Now dePaola is famous for his art and storytelling. His childhood dream has come true. He says he always knew it would.

Tomie dePaola

Author and Artist

Here's how author and artist Tomie dePaola puts stories together in his studio.

Tomie dePaola gets ideas for his books from everywhere. Sometimes the ideas come from his childhood. At other times, they come right out of his imagination.

Perhaps because drawing was his first love, he gets some story ideas from pictures he draws. Strega Nona was a character he started doodling one day, just for fun. He decided that she was just right for a story about a woman with a special pasta pot.

Even if a story idea comes from a drawing, Mr. dePaola doesn't do the pictures first. He works out the story first because he thinks that the story is more important. The pictures add to the story.

Tomie dePaola tries to create stories and art that mean a lot to children. He wants to be part of their lives. He says, "I share my feelings with children, and I think they appreciate that."

Tomie dePaola's
Tips to Young Authors and Artists

1 Decide who to write about. Will your characters be people or animals?

2 Decide what you want your characters to do. Will it be real or make-believe? Will it be funny, sad, or scary?

3 As you write your story, draw pictures that tell the story as much as the words do.

Think About Reading

1. What is inside the big egg that Little Grunt brings home?

2. Why does George have to leave?

3. Why do you think George comes back to save Little Grunt and the rest of the Grunts?

4. When does the story take place? How do the pictures help you understand the setting and the characters?

5. How do you think Tomie dePaola got the idea for this story?

Write a Poem

Write the letters of George's name down the page like this.

G

E

O

R

G

E

Use each letter to begin a word or group of words that tells about George. For example, you might use the first letter *G* to begin *Gentle* or *Giant-sized* or *Good to his friends.*

Literature Circle

Did the story end the way you expected it to? Think of another ending for the story. How would the story change to fit the new ending?

Author
Tomie dePaola

Readers all over the world love Tomie dePaola's books. He gets nearly 100,000 fan letters every year. His fans like knowing lots of facts about Tomie. For example, they like to know that his favorite color is white and his favorite food is popcorn. They also like to know that he has four dogs named Madison, Moffat, Morgan, and Markus.

More Books by
Tomie dePaola

- *The Cloud Book*
- *Charlie Needs a Cloak*
- *The Art Lesson*

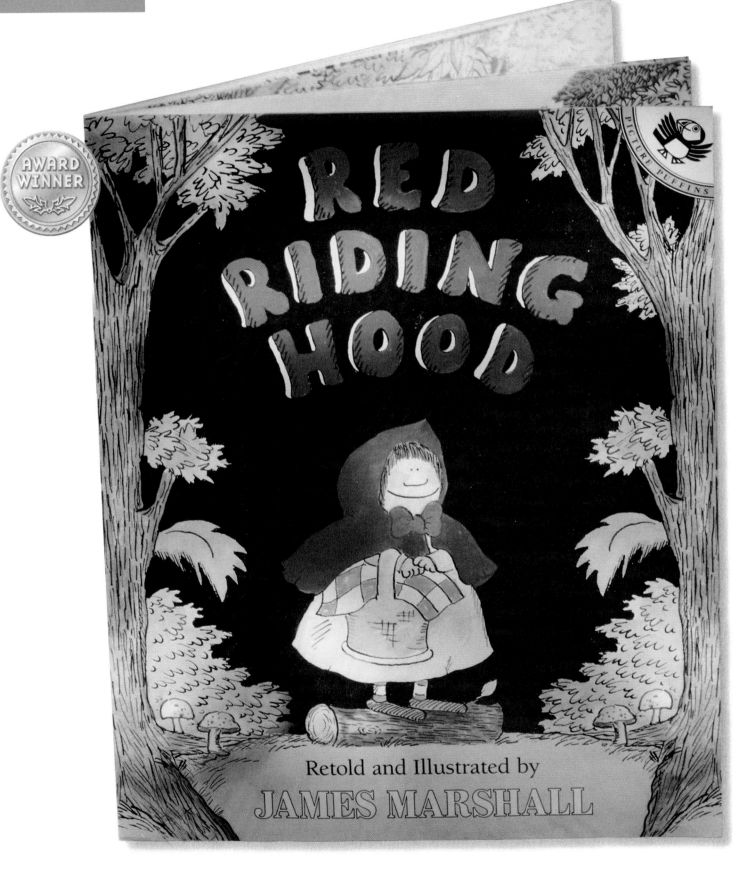

AWARD WINNER

PICTURE PUFFINS

RED RIDING HOOD

Retold and Illustrated by

JAMES MARSHALL

A long time ago
in a simple cottage
beside the deep, dark woods,
there lived a pretty child
called Red Riding Hood.
She was kind and considerate,
and everybody loved her.

One afternoon
Red Riding Hood's mother called to her.
"Granny isn't feeling up to snuff today,"
she said, "so I've baked
her favorite custard
as a little surprise.
Be a good girl and
take it to her, will you?"
Red Riding Hood was delighted.
She loved going to Granny's—
even though it meant crossing
the deep, dark woods.

93

98

When the custard
had cooled, Red Riding Hood's
mother wrapped it up
and put it in a basket.
"Now, whatever you do,"
she said,
"go straight to Granny's,
do not tarry,
do not speak
to any strangers."
"Yes, Mama,"
said Red Riding Hood.

Before long she was
in the deepest part of the woods.
"Oooh," she said. "This is scary."

Suddenly a large wolf appeared.
"Good afternoon, my dear,"
he said.
"Care to stop for a little chat?"
"Oh, gracious me,"
said Red Riding Hood.
"Mama said not to speak
to any strangers."

But the wolf had *such*
charming manners.
"And where are you going,
sweet thing?" he said.
"I'm on my way to visit Granny,
who lives in the pretty yellow house
on the other side of the woods,"
said Red Riding Hood.
"She's feeling poorly,
and I'm taking her a surprise."
"You don't say," said the wolf.
Just then he had a delightful idea.
No reason why I can't eat them *both*,
he thought.
"Allow me to escort you," he said.
"You never know what might be
lurking about."
"You're too kind," said Red Riding Hood.

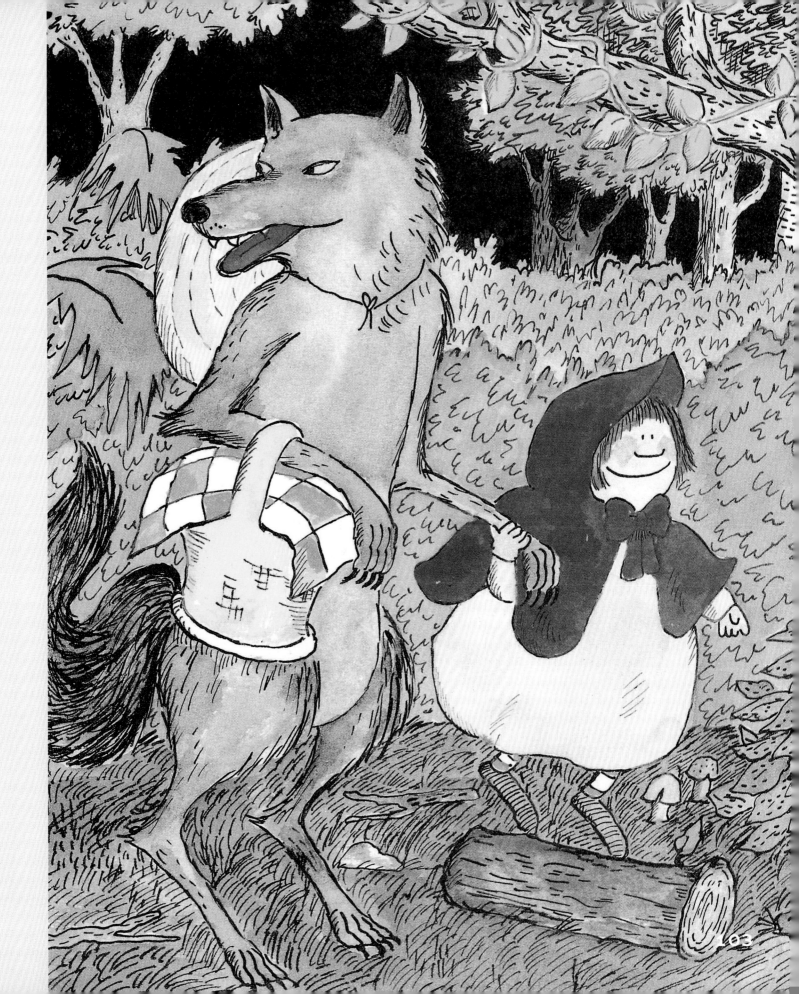

103

Beyond the forest they came
to a patch of sunflowers.
"Why not pick a few?"
suggested the wolf.
"Grannies *love* flowers,
you know."
But while Red Riding Hood was
picking a pretty bouquet,
the clever wolf hurried on ahead
to Granny's house.

"Who is it?"
called out Granny.
"It is I, your delicious—er—
darling granddaughter,"
said the wolf
in a high voice.
"The door is unlocked,"
said Granny.

"Surprise!"
cried the wolf.
Granny was furious at
having her reading interrupted.
"Get out of here,
you horrid thing!"
she cried.

But the wolf gobbled her right up.
He didn't even bother to chew.
"Tasty," he said, patting his belly,
"so tasty."
Just then he heard footsteps
on the garden path.
"Here comes dessert!"
And losing no time, he put on
Granny's cap and glasses,
jumped into bed, and pulled up the covers.

"Who is it?"
he called out
in his sweetest granny voice.
"It is I, your little granddaughter,"
said Red Riding Hood.
"The door is unlocked,"
said the wolf.

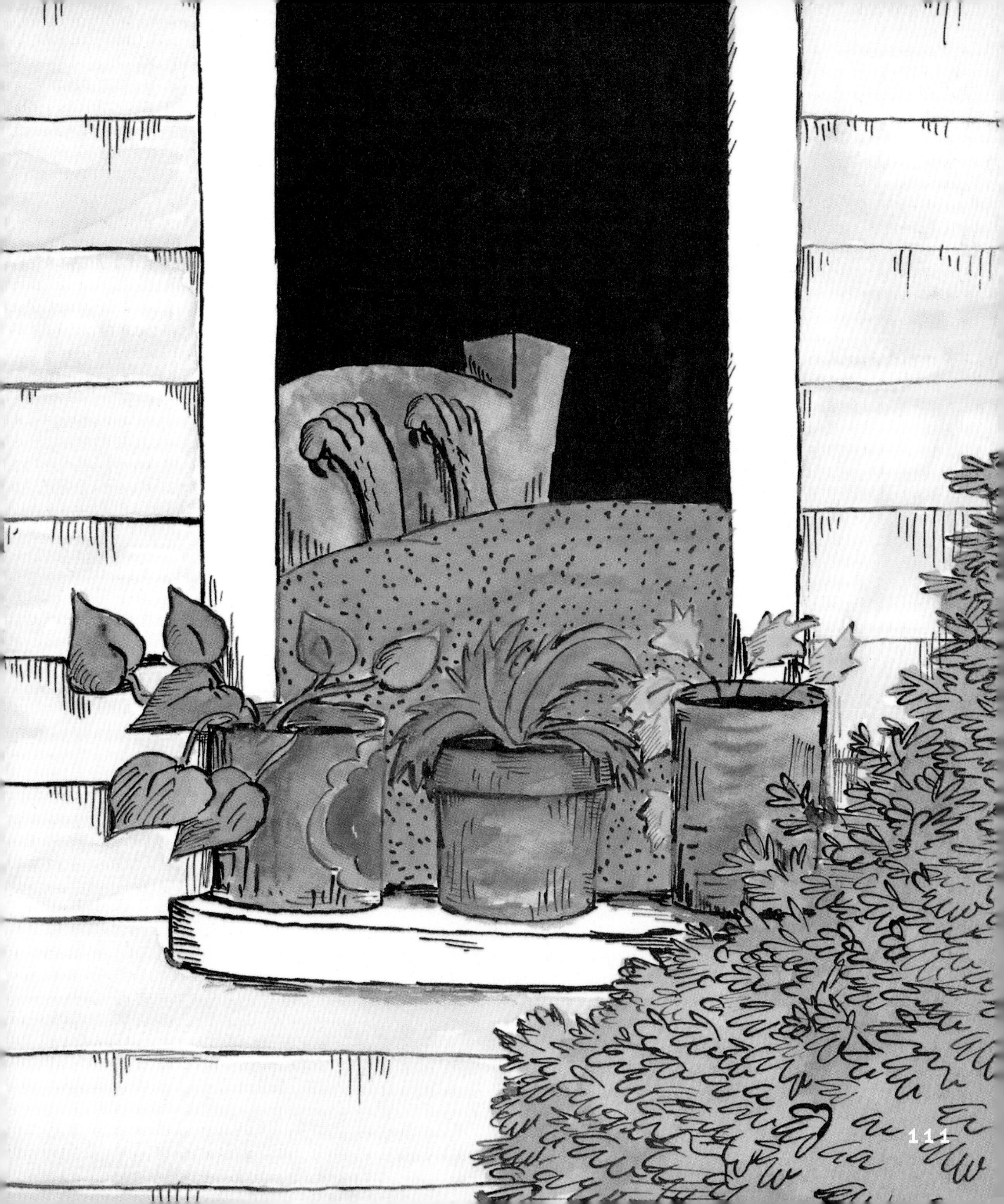

Red Riding Hood was distressed
at seeing her grandmother so changed.
"Why, Granny," she said,
"what big eyes you have."
"The better to see you, my dear," said the wolf.
"And Granny, what long arms you have."
"The better to hug you, my dear," said the wolf.
"And Granny, what big teeth you have."

"THE BETTER TO EAT YOU, MY DEAR!"
cried the wolf.

And he gobbled her right up.
"I'm so wicked," he said. "*So* wicked."
But really he was
enormously pleased with himself.
And having enjoyed such a
heavy meal, he was soon snoring away.
A hunter passing by was alarmed
by the frightful racket.
"That doesn't sound like Granny!"
he said.

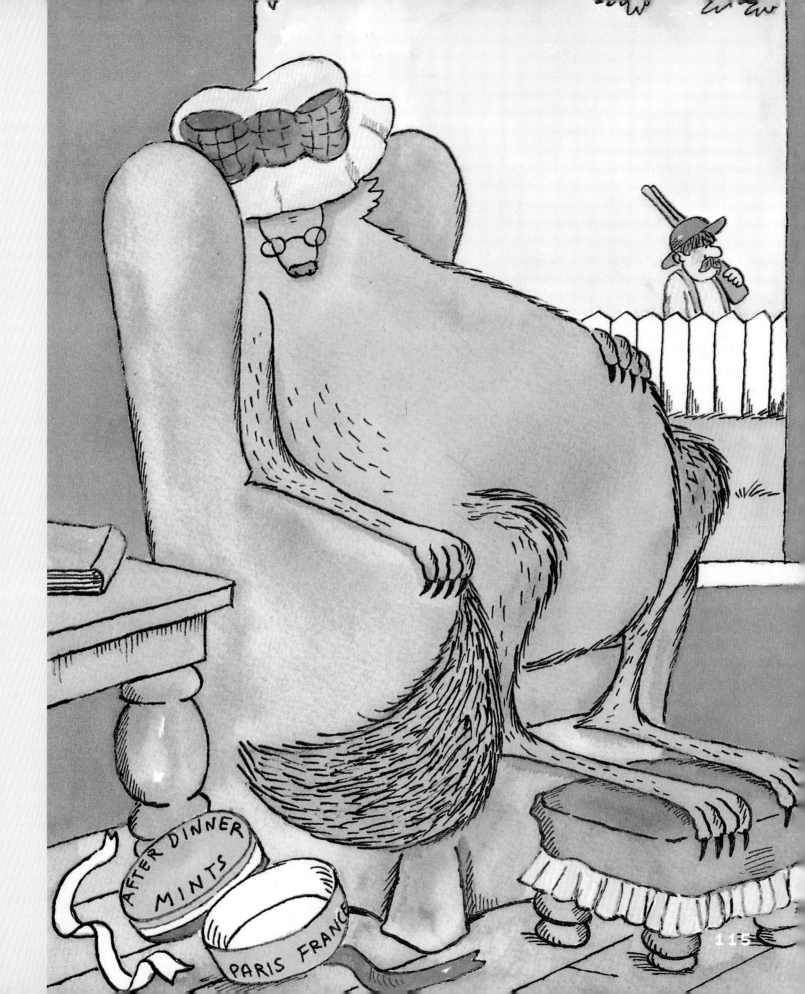

AFTER DINNER MINTS

PARIS FRANCE

115

And so the brave hunter
jumped in the window,
killed the sleeping wolf,
and cut him open.
Out jumped Granny and Red Riding Hood.
"We're ever so grateful,"
said Red Riding Hood.
"That wicked wolf won't trouble
you again," said the hunter.
"It was so dark in there I couldn't read a *word*,"
said Granny.
Red Riding Hood promised never,
ever to speak to another stranger,
charming manners or not.

And she never did.

And Still More Tales

People have been telling tales like *Little Red Riding Hood* for hundreds of years. Sometimes they change the words or pictures to make the tale even more interesting or funny. Sometimes the setting is changed to show how different people live. A big bad wolf might become a city cat or a fox! Cinderella can even be a boy!

Here are some different tellings of favorite tales.

LITTLE RED RIDING HOOD

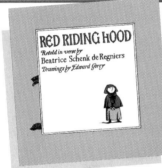

A Rhyming Tale

A City Tale

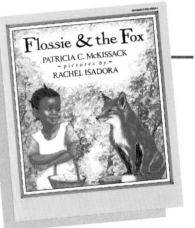

A Southern Tale

THE FROG PRINCE

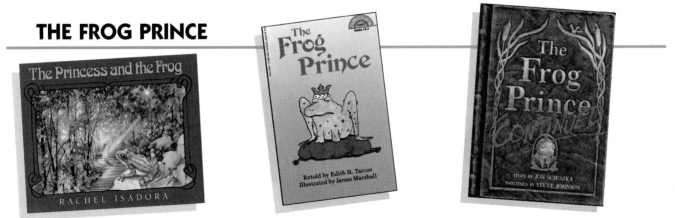

A Beautiful Tale

A Funny Tale

The Happily-Ever-After Tale

CINDERELLA

The Stepsister's Tale

A Sports Tale

A Chinese Tale

JACK AND THE BEANSTALK

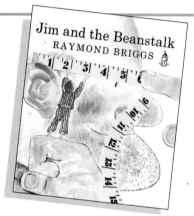

The Classic Tale

An Old-Fashioned Tale

The Tale Continues

THE MOUSE BRIDE

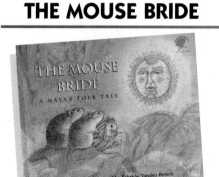

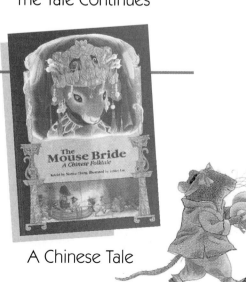

A Mayan Tale

A Japanese Tale

A Chinese Tale

THINK ABOUT READING

1. Why does Red Riding Hood's mother ask her to go to Granny's house?

2. Why does the wolf offer to walk through the woods with Red Riding Hood?

3. Why do you think the wolf doesn't just wait inside the door to surprise Red Riding Hood?

4. In the end Red Riding Hood learns not to speak to strangers. What might have happened if she had remembered that rule on her way to Granny's house?

5. Which other books on pages 118 and 119 tell the same tale you just read?

WRITE QUESTIONS

Suppose you could talk with Red Riding Hood. What else would you want to know about her? Write three questions you would ask Red Riding Hood.

LITERATURE CIRCLE

Which of the books in "And Still More Tales" have you read? Why do you think people tell these stories over and over? Why do you think some authors make changes in these old stories?

AUTHOR
JAMES MARSHALL

When James Marshall was a boy, he didn't like toast. He knew just what to do with it. He hid it in his closet! Think about a closet full of toast. That's a funny picture. Funny pictures like that give James Marshall his ideas for books. Once he sees something funny in his mind, he adds words and makes a story.

More Books by James Marshall

- *Miss Nelson Is Missing* (with Harry Allard)
- *Fox Outfoxed*
- *The Cut-Ups Carry On*

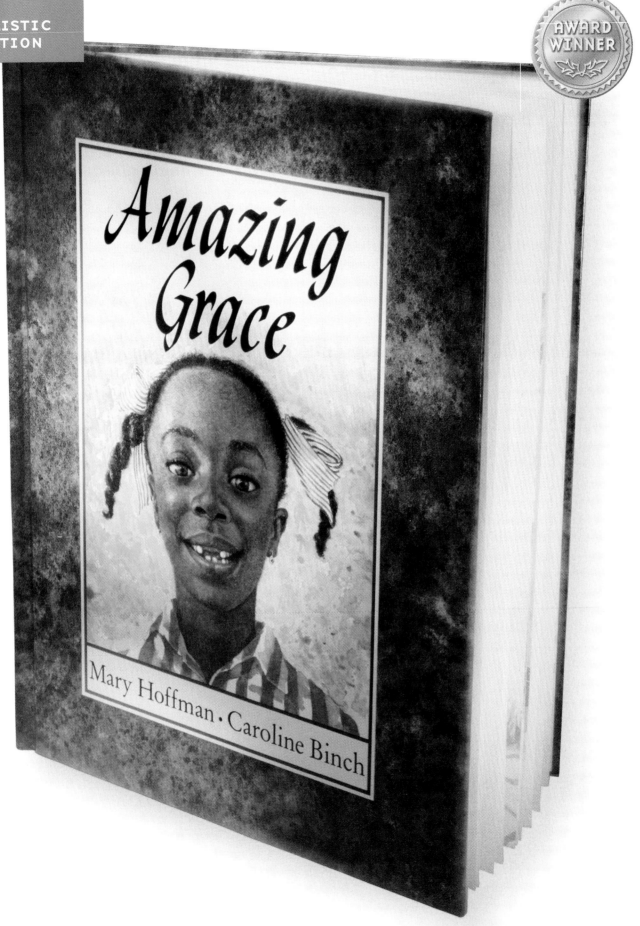

Grace was a girl who loved stories.

She didn't mind if they were read to her or told to her or made up in her own head. She didn't care if they were in books or movies or out of Nana's long memory. Grace just loved stories.

After she had heard them, and sometimes while they were still going on, Grace would act them out. And she always gave herself the most exciting part.

Grace went into battle as Joan of Arc ...

and wove a wicked web as Anansi the Spider.

She hid inside the wooden horse at the gates of Troy....

She went exploring for lost kingdoms....

She sailed the seven seas
with a peg leg and a parrot.

She was Hiawatha, sitting by
the shining Big-Sea-Water …

and Mowgli in the backyard jungle.

Most of all Grace loved to act out adventure stories and fairy tales. When there was no one else around, Grace played all the parts herself.

She set out to seek her fortune, with no companion but her trusty cat—and found a city with streets paved in gold.

Or she was Aladdin, rubbing his magic lamp to make the genie appear.

Sometimes she could get Ma and Nana to join in, when they weren't too busy.

Then she was Doctor Grace and their lives were in her hands.

One day Grace's teacher said they would do the play *Peter Pan.* Grace knew who she wanted to be.

When she raised her hand, Raj said, "You can't be Peter—that's a boy's name."

But Grace kept her hand up.

"You can't be Peter Pan," whispered Natalie. "He isn't black." But Grace kept her hand up.

"All right," said the teacher. "Lots of you want to be Peter Pan, so we'll have auditions next week to choose parts." She gave them words to learn.

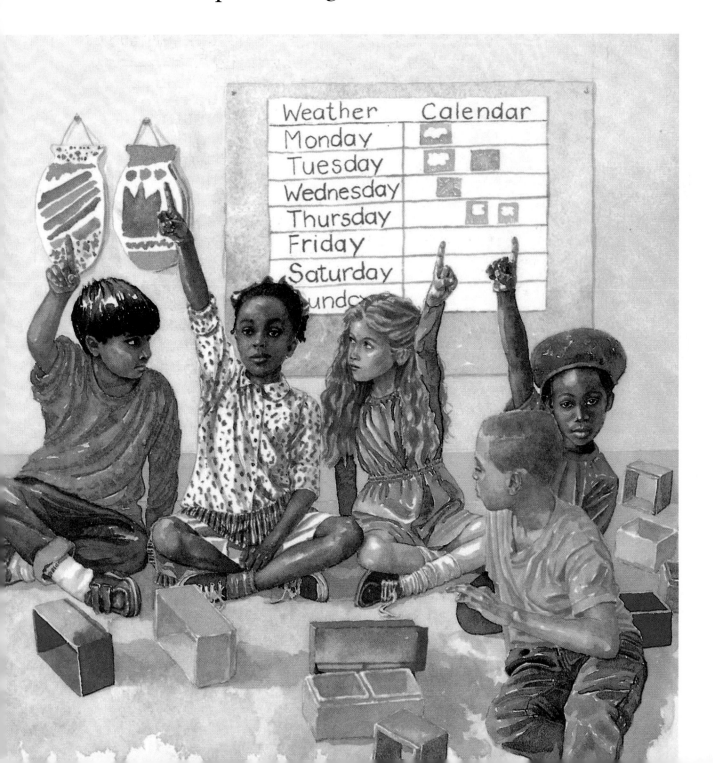

When Grace got home,
she seemed sad.

"What's the matter?"
asked Ma.

"Raj said I can't be
Peter Pan because I'm a girl."

"That just shows what Raj
knows," said Ma. "A girl
can be Peter Pan if she
wants to."

Grace cheered up, then later she remembered something else. "Natalie says I can't be Peter Pan because I'm black," she said.

Ma looked angry. But before she could speak, Nana said, "It seems that Natalie is another one who don't know nothing. You can be anything you want, Grace, if you put your mind to it."

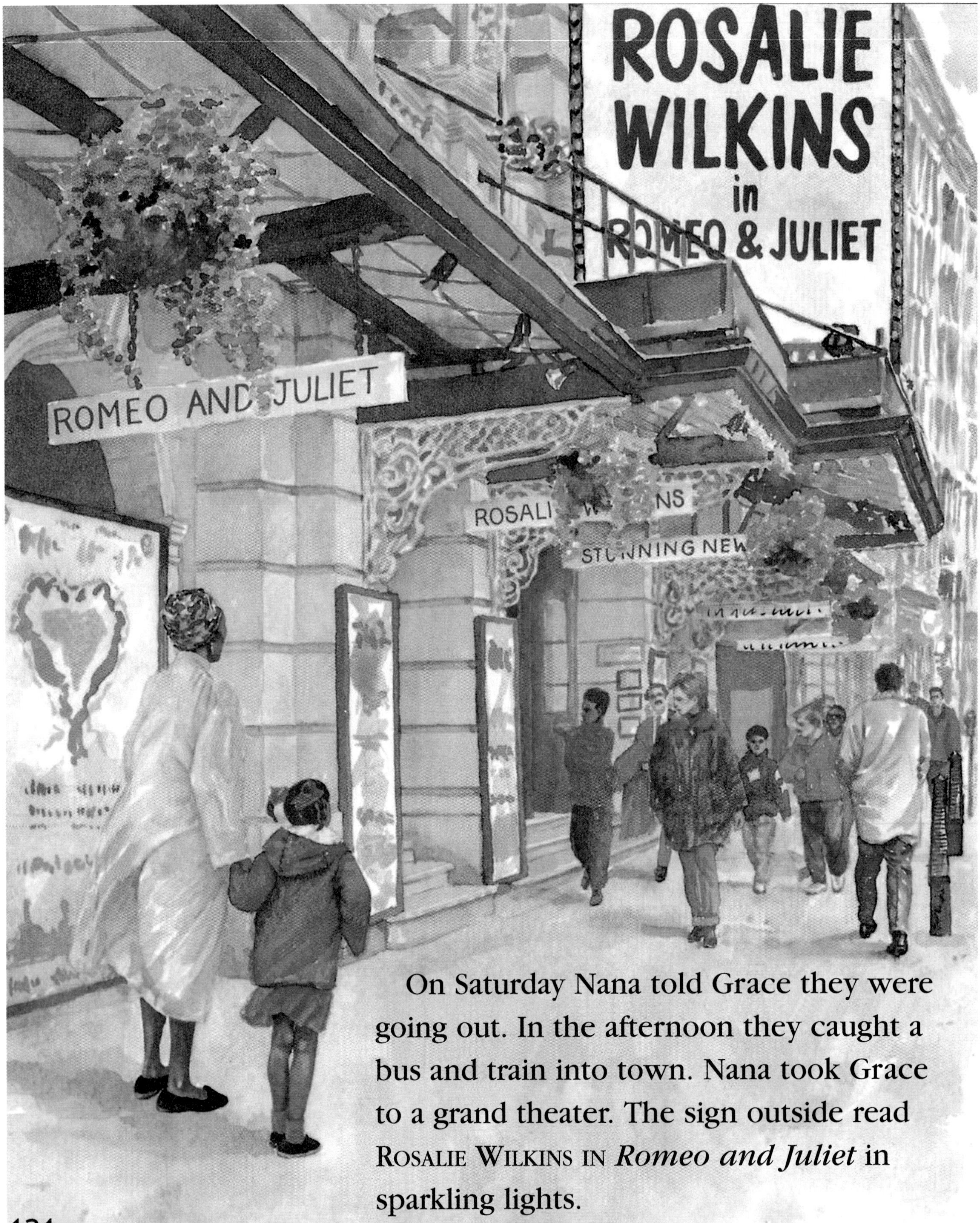

ROSALIE
WILKINS
in
ROMEO & JULIET

ROMEO AND JULIET

ROSALIE W KINS

STUNNING NEW

On Saturday Nana told Grace they were going out. In the afternoon they caught a bus and train into town. Nana took Grace to a grand theater. The sign outside read ROSALIE WILKINS IN *Romeo and Juliet* in sparkling lights.

"Are we going to the ballet, Nana?" asked Grace.

"We are, honey, but first I want you to look at this picture."

Grace looked up and saw a beautiful young ballerina in a tutu. Above the dancer it said STUNNING NEW JULIET.

"That one is little Rosalie from back home in Trinidad," said Nana. "Her granny and me, we grew up together on the island. She's always asking me do I want tickets to see her Rosalie dance—so this time I said yes."

After the ballet Grace played the part of Juliet,
dancing around her room in her imaginary tutu.
I can be anything I want, she thought.

On Monday the class met for auditions to choose who was best for each part.

When it was Grace's turn to be Peter, she knew exactly what to do and all the words to say—she had been Peter Pan all weekend. She took a deep breath and imagined herself flying.

When it was time to vote, the class chose Raj to be Captain Hook and Natalie to be Wendy. There was no doubt who would be Peter Pan. *Everyone* voted for Grace.

"You were fantastic!" whispered Natalie.

The play was a big success and Grace was an amazing Peter Pan.

After it was all over, she said, "I feel as if I could fly all the way home!"

"You probably could," said Ma.

"Yes," said Nana. "If Grace put her mind to it, she can do anything she want."

THEATER PROGRAM

An Amazing Peter Pan

Larry Malvern was the actor chosen to play Peter Pan when the musical was performed by a theater company in Pennsylvania.

Here is a page from the play program and some photographs from the show.

The Cast List

142

Wendy, Michael, and the Lost Boys

Tinkerbell and Peter Pan

Captain Hook

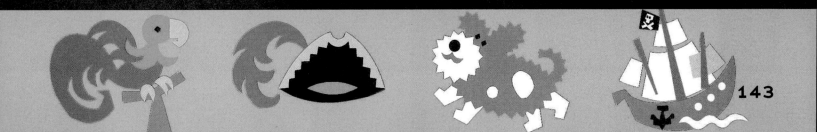

Think About Reading

Think about *Amazing Grace*. Answer the questions in the story map. Do your work on another sheet of paper.

Characters

1. Who is the main character?
2. What does she like to do?

Problem

3. What part does Grace want in the play?
4. Why do her friends say Grace can't have that part?

Ending

5. Who gets the part of Peter Pan in the play?
6. What does Grace learn?

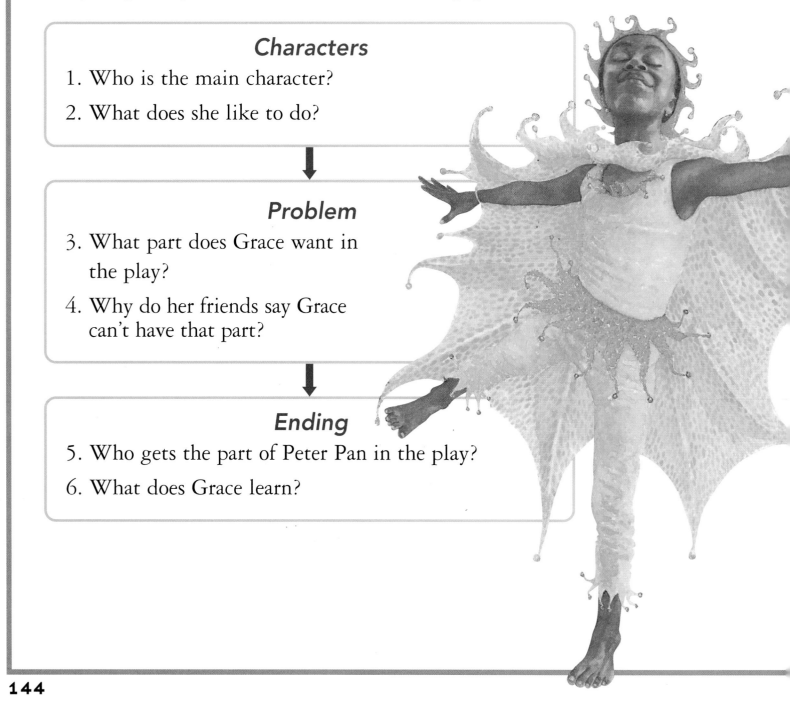

Write a Journal Entry

How do you think Grace feels after being in the play? What details do you think she remembers? What plans do you think she makes? Put yourself in Grace's place and write a journal entry.

Literature Circle

Grace auditioned for the part of Peter Pan even though her classmates told her the part was not right for her. What does this tell you about Grace? What kind of person is she? Would you like to have her for a friend? Why?

Illustrator
Caroline Binch

When Caroline Binch works, she gets to do two things she enjoys-she draws pictures and she travels. She especially likes to travel to Trinidad, the Caribbean island where Grace's Ma and Nana once lived. Binch also likes making up her own stories. Sometimes she writes the books she illustrates.

More Books Illustrated by
Caroline Binch

- *Gregory Cool* (She's the author, too.)
- *Boundless Grace*
- *Down by the River*

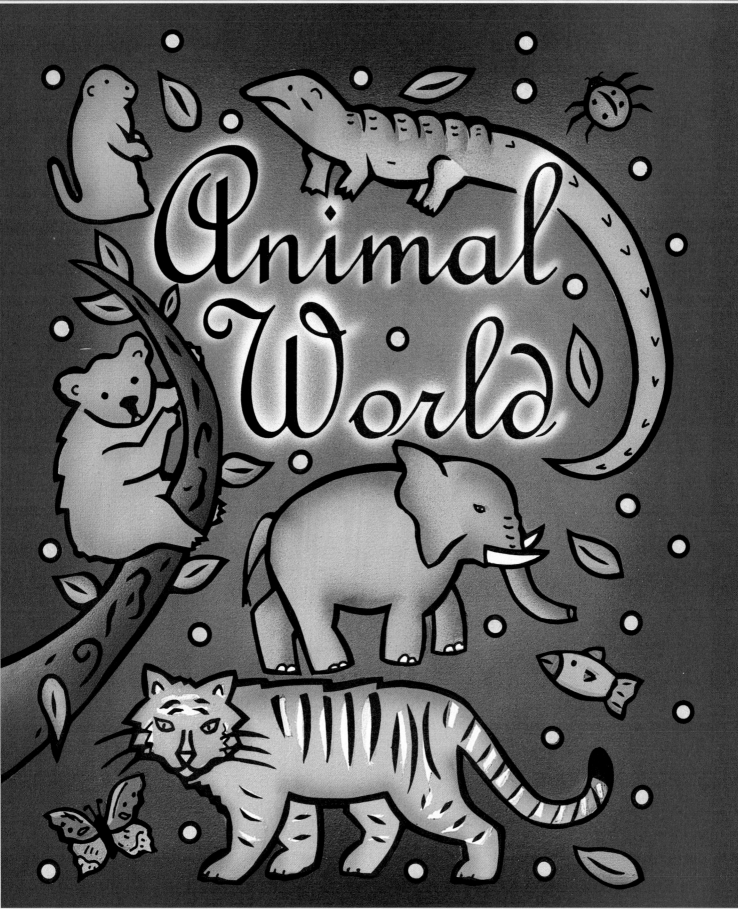

Animal World

Animal World

THEME

We use information to understand the interdependence of people and animals.

www.scholastic.com

Visit the kids' area of **www.scholastic.com** for the latest news about your favorite Scholastic books. You'll find sneak previews of new books, interviews with authors and illustrators, and lots of other great stuff!

Stellaluna **150**
by Janell Cannon

Balto: The Dog Who Saved Nome . . **194**
by Margaret Davidson

Puppygarten Star **210**

Ibis: A True Whale Story **214**
by John Himmelman

Working with Whales **232**

When the Monkeys Came Back **236**
by Kristine L. Franklin

MENTOR

Zoo Curator **Lisa Stevens** **258**

from **How Artists See Animals** **264**
by Colleen Carroll

Animal Messengers **276**

GLOSSARY **426**

UNIT 5

Welcome to

LITERACY PLACE

Learn at a Zoo

We use information
to understand
the interdependence
of people and animals.

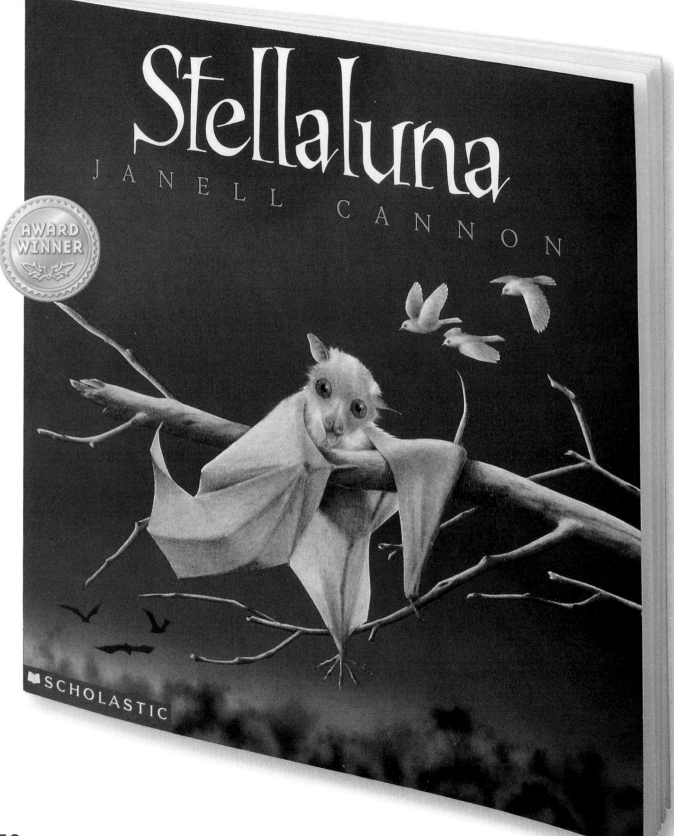

AWARD WINNER

Stellaluna

JANELL CANNON

SCHOLASTIC

In a warm and sultry forest far, far away, there once lived a mother fruit bat and her new baby.

Oh, how Mother Bat loved her soft tiny baby. "I'll name you Stellaluna," she crooned.

Each night, Mother Bat would carry Stellaluna clutched to her breast as she flew out to search for food.

One night, as Mother Bat followed the heavy scent of ripe fruit, an owl spied her. On silent wings the powerful bird swooped down upon the bats.

Dodging and shrieking, Mother Bat tried to escape, but the owl struck again and again, knocking Stellaluna into the air. Her baby wings were as limp and useless as wet paper.

Down, down she went, faster and faster, into the forest below.

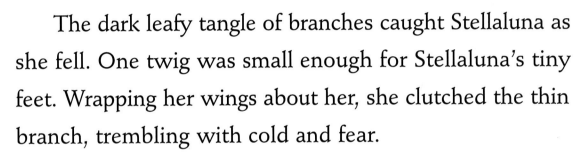

The dark leafy tangle of branches caught Stellaluna as she fell. One twig was small enough for Stellaluna's tiny feet. Wrapping her wings about her, she clutched the thin branch, trembling with cold and fear.

"Mother," Stellaluna squeaked. "Where are you?"

By daybreak, the baby bat could hold on no longer. Down, down again she dropped.

Flump! Stellaluna landed headfirst in a soft downy nest, startling the three baby birds who lived there.

Stellaluna quickly clambered from the nest and hung out of sight below it. She listened to the babble of the three birds.

"What was *that*?" cried Flap.

"I don't know, but it's hanging by its feet," chirped Flitter.

"Shhh! Here comes Mama," hissed Pip.

Many, many times that day Mama Bird flew away, always returning with food for her babies.

Stellaluna was terribly hungry—but *not* for the crawly things Mama Bird brought.

Finally, though, the little bat could bear it no longer. She climbed into the nest, closed her eyes, and opened her mouth.

Plop! In dropped a big green grasshopper!

Stellaluna learned to be like the birds. She stayed awake all day and slept at night. She ate bugs even though they tasted awful. Her bat ways were quickly disappearing. Except for one thing: Stellaluna still liked to sleep hanging by her feet.

Once, when Mama was away, the curious baby birds decided to try it, too. When Mama Bird came home she saw eight tiny feet gripping the edge of the nest.

"Eeeek!" she cried. "Get back up here this instant! You're going to fall and break your necks!"

The birds clambered back into the nest, but Mama Bird stopped Stellaluna. "You are teaching my children to do bad things. I will not let you back into this nest unless you promise to obey all the rules of this house."

Stellaluna promised. She ate bugs without making faces. She slept in the nest at night. And she didn't hang by her feet. Stellaluna behaved as a good bird should.

All the babies grew quickly. Soon the nest became crowded.

Mama Bird told them it was time to learn to fly. One by one, Pip, Flitter, Flap, and Stellaluna jumped from the nest.

Their wings worked!

I'm just like them, thought Stellaluna. I can fly, too.

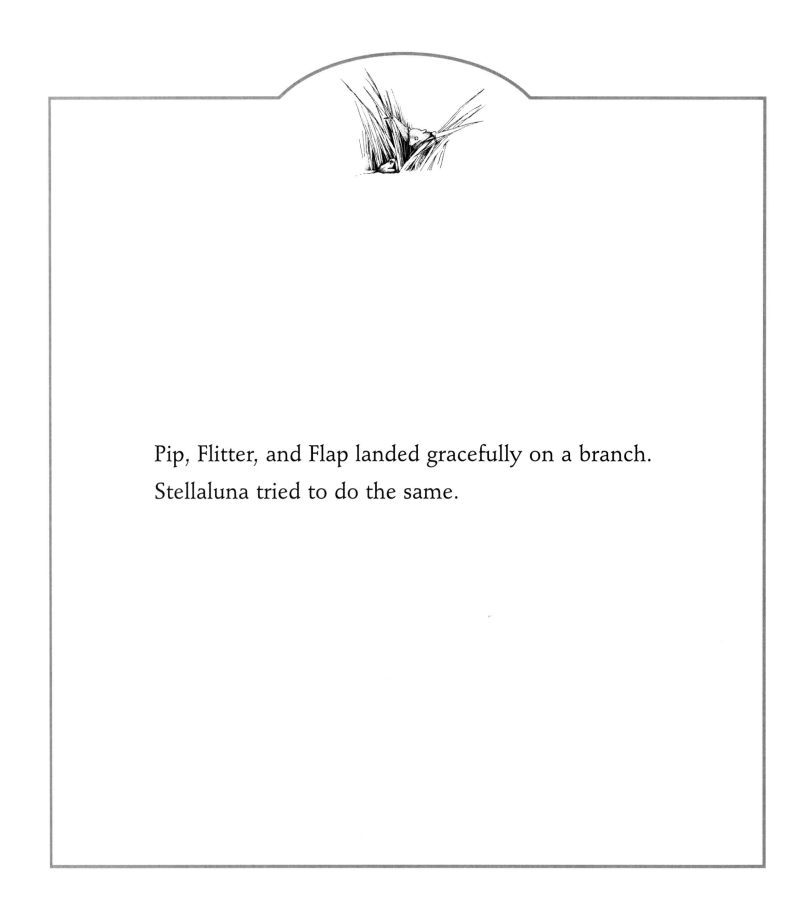

Pip, Flitter, and Flap landed gracefully on a branch.
Stellaluna tried to do the same.

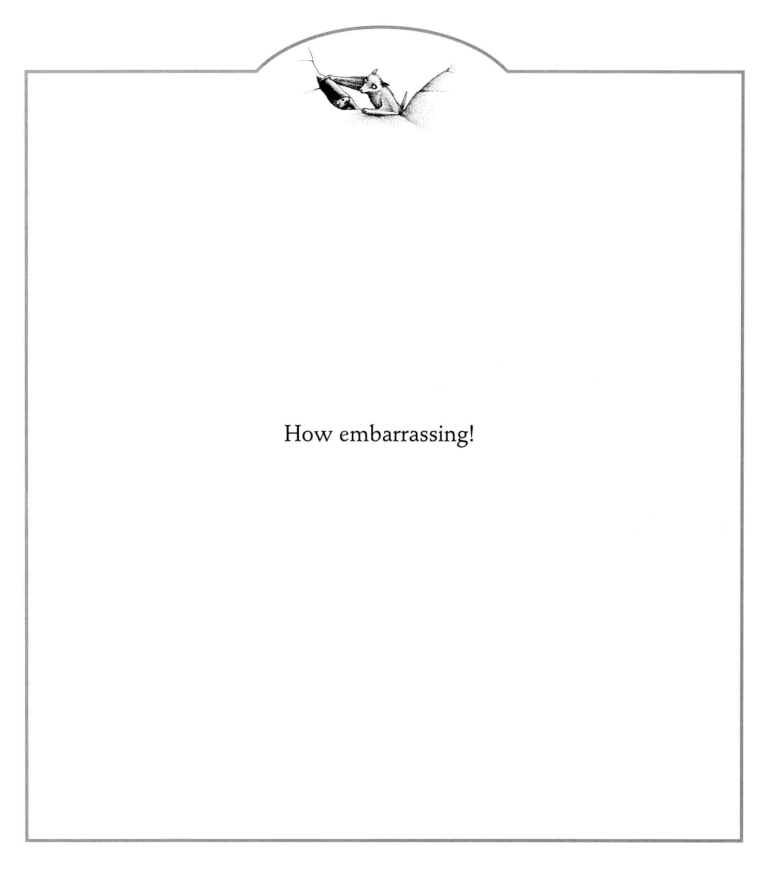

How embarrassing!

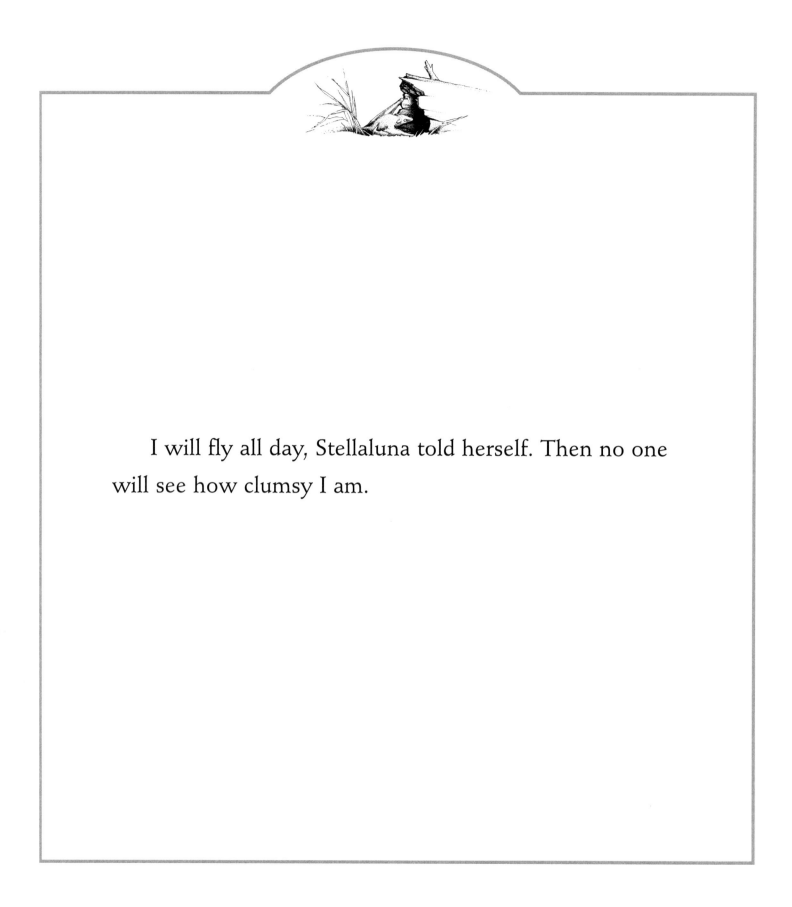

I will fly all day, Stellaluna told herself. Then no one will see how clumsy I am.

The next day, Pip, Flitter, Flap, and Stellaluna went flying far from home. They flew for hours, exercising their new wings.

"The sun is setting," warned Flitter.

"We had better go home or we will get lost in the dark," said Flap.

But Stellaluna had flown far ahead and was nowhere to be seen. The three anxious birds went home without her.

173

All alone Stellaluna flew and flew until her wings ached and she dropped into a tree. "I promised not to hang by my feet," Stellaluna sighed. So she hung by her thumbs and soon fell asleep.

She didn't hear the soft sound of wings coming near.

"Hey!" a loud voice said. "Why are you hanging upside down?"

Stellaluna's eyes opened wide. She saw a most peculiar face. "I'm not upside down, *you* are!" Stellaluna said.

"Ah, but you're a *bat*. Bats hang by their feet. You are hanging by your thumbs, so that makes you *upside down!*" the creature said. "I'm a bat. I am hanging by my feet. That makes me *right side up!*"

Stellaluna was confused. "Mama Bird told me I was upside down. She said I was wrong . . ."

"Wrong for a bird, maybe, but not for a bat."

More bats gathered around to see the strange young bat who behaved like a bird. Stellaluna told them her story.

"You ate *b-bugs*?" stuttered one.

"You slept at *night*?" gasped another.

"How very strange," they all murmured.

"Wait! Wait! Let me look at this child." A bat pushed through the crowd. "An *owl* attacked you?" she asked. Sniffing Stellaluna's fur, she whispered, "You are *Stellaluna*. You are my baby."

"You escaped the owl?" cried Stellaluna. "You survived?"

"Yes," said Mother Bat as she wrapped her wings around Stellaluna. "Come with me and I'll show you where to find the most delicious fruit. You'll never have to eat another bug as long as you live."

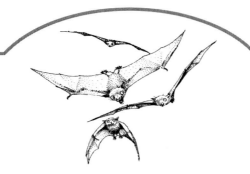

"But it's nighttime," Stellaluna squeaked. "We can't fly in the dark or we will crash into trees."

"We're bats," said Mother Bat. "We can see in darkness. Come with us."

Stellaluna was afraid, but she let go of the tree and dropped into the deep blue sky.

Stellaluna *could* see. She felt as though rays of light shone from her eyes. She was able to see everything in her path.

Soon the bats found a mango tree, and Stellaluna ate as much of the fruit as she could hold.

"I'll never eat another bug as long as I live," cheered Stellaluna as she stuffed herself full. "I must tell Pip, Flitter, and Flap!"

The next day Stellaluna went to visit the birds.

"Come with me and meet my bat family," said Stellaluna.

"Okay, let's go," agreed Pip.

"They hang by their feet and they fly at night and they eat the best food in the world," Stellaluna explained to the birds on the way.

As the birds flew among the bats, Flap said, "I feel upside down here."

So the birds hung by their feet.

"Wait until dark," Stellaluna said excitedly. "We will fly at night."

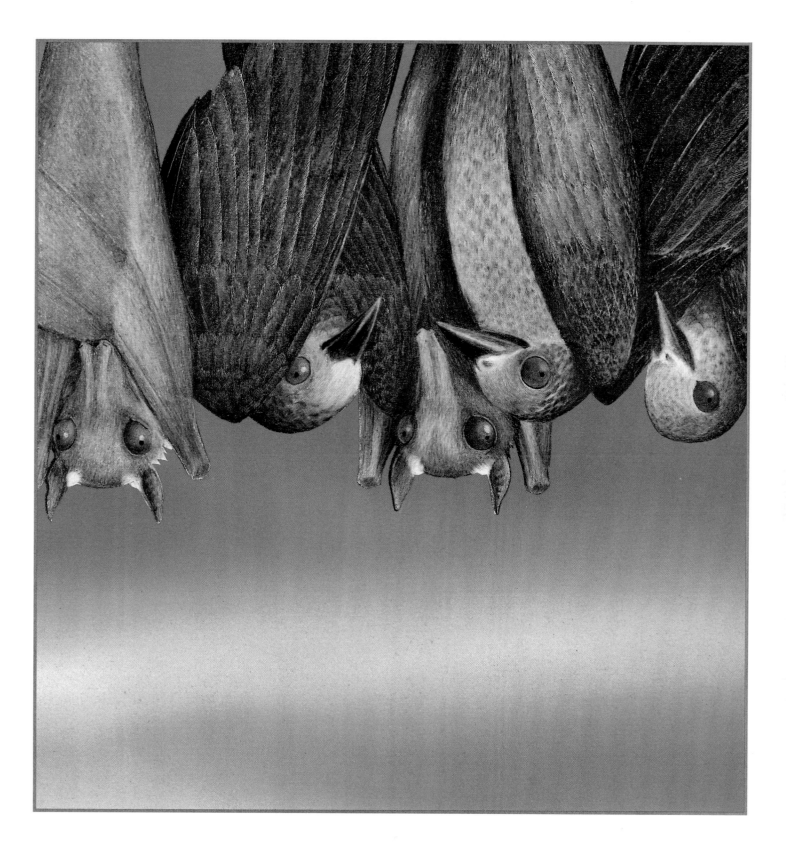

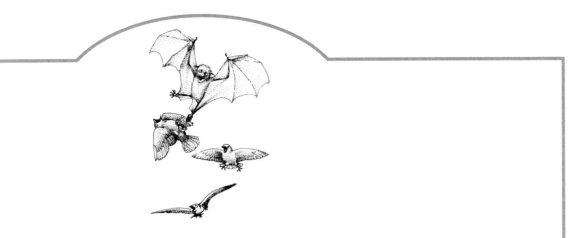

When night came Stellaluna flew away. Pip, Flitter, and Flap leapt from the tree to follow her.

"I can't see a thing!" yelled Pip.

"Neither can I," howled Flitter.

"Aaeee!" shrieked Flap.

"They're going to crash," gasped Stellaluna. "I must rescue them!"

Stellaluna swooped about, grabbing her friends in the air. She lifted them to a tree, and the birds grasped a branch. Stellaluna hung from the limb above them.

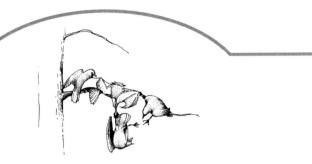

"We're safe," said Stellaluna. Then she sighed. "I wish you could see in the dark, too."

"We wish you could land on your feet," Flitter replied. Pip and Flap nodded.

They perched in silence for a long time.

"How can we be so different and feel so much alike?" mused Flitter.

"And how can we feel so different and be so much alike?" wondered Pip.

"I think this is quite a mystery," Flap chirped.

"I agree," said Stellaluna. "But we're friends. And that's a fact."

Think About Reading

1. Where does Stellaluna finally land after the owl attacks her mother?

2. What does Stellaluna do to be like a bird?

3. How do you think Stellaluna feels when she finds out that one of the bats is her mother?

4. Look at the picture on page 161. How can you tell from the picture that the birds and Stellaluna are make-believe characters?

5. Do you think that Stellaluna will go on being friends with Pip, Flitter, and Flap? Why or why not?

Write a Comparison

Stellaluna and her bird friends—Pip, Flitter, and Flap—know that they are different in many ways. Write a paragraph telling how bats and birds are different. Draw a picture to go with your paragraph.

Literature Circle

What do you think the author wants *Stellaluna* readers to learn about bats? What do you think she wants readers to learn about people? Talk about your ideas.

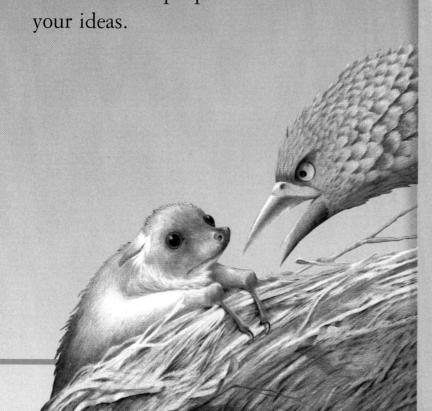

Author
JANELL CANNON

Janell Cannon likes unusual animals. Of course, her favorite animals are bats. She also likes spiders, snakes, and Komodo dragons. (They're not really dragons! They're the world's biggest lizards.) She also likes imaginary animals. Cannon's own pets are not too unusual, though. She has a cat and a parrot.

MORE BOOKS BY
JANELL CANNON

- *Verdi*
- *Trupp: A Fuzzhead Tail*

193

BALTO

The Dog Who Saved Nome

By Margaret Davidson

Illustrated by Cathie Bleck

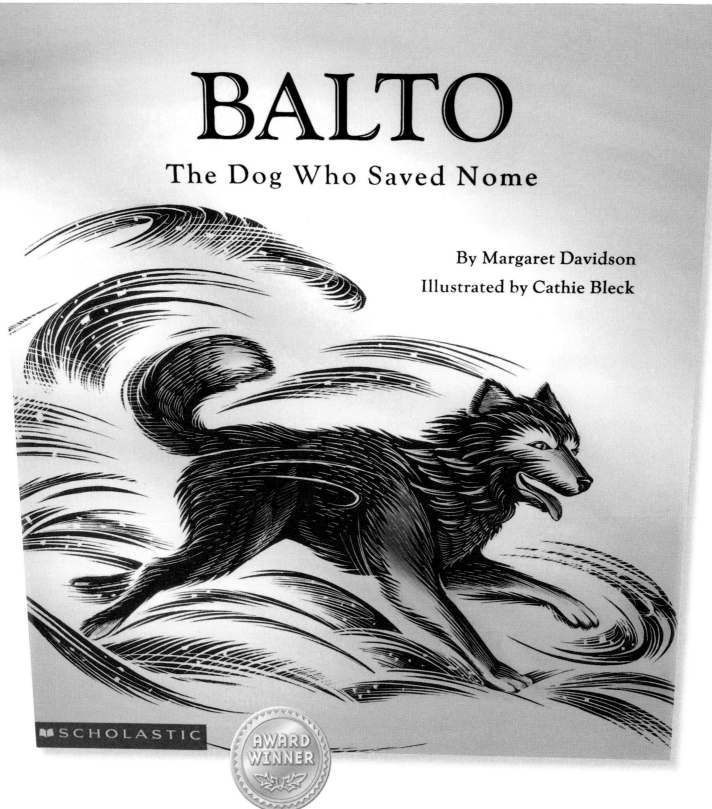

AWARD WINNER

"THIS IS NOME, ALASKA. REPEAT. THIS IS NOME, ALASKA. WE NEED HELP. FAST…"

A man bent over the machine in the Nome telegraph office. Again and again he pressed down the signal key. *Click-click-clack … Clack-click-clack …* He was sending a message to the town of Anchorage, Alaska, 800 miles to the south.

Click-click-clack … Clack-click-clack … The Anchorage telegraph operator wrote down the message. The news was very bad.

A terrible sickness had broken out in the Nome area—a disease called diphtheria. Some people had already died of it. Many more would die if they weren't treated soon.

There was no medicine to treat diphtheria in Nome. The medicine they needed would have to come from Anchorage—800 miles away—through a wild wind and snow storm. The storm was so bad that airplanes couldn't fly through it. Trains couldn't get through either. Nome was very near the sea, but the sea was frozen solid. And the road from the south was completely blocked by deep drifts of snow.

There was only one way to get the medicine from Anchorage to Nome—by dogsled.

The medicine was packed in a box and sent north by train—as far as a train could go on the snowy tracks. It was still more than 600 miles south of Nome. From now on teams of dogs would have to take it the rest of the way.

The teams were ready. The first team pushed north through the storm to a little town. There a second team was waiting. It went on to another small town where a third team was ready to take the medicine on north.

At first the teams managed to go many miles before they grew tired. But the storm was growing worse by the minute. Finally Charlie Olson's team staggered into the little village of Bluff—60 miles south of Nome. They had only gone 20 miles, yet Olson and the dogs were almost frozen and completely worn out.

Gunnar Kasson and his team were waiting in Bluff. The wind screamed through the little town. The snow was piling up deeper and deeper on the ground. It was 30 degrees *below* zero Fahrenheit outside now. And the temperature was falling fast.

"It's no use trying to go out in *that*," Charlie Olson said. "I almost didn't make it. You and the dogs will freeze solid before you get half way."

But Kasson knew how important the medicine was. He knew that hundreds—maybe thousands—of people would die if they didn't get the medicine soon. Besides, he knew he didn't have to go all the way. Another team was waiting 40 miles north in the little village of Safety. That team would take the medicine the last 20 miles to Nome.

Quickly Gunnar Kasson hitched up his team of dogs. And at the head of the long line he put his lead dog, Balto.

Balto was a mixed-breed. He was half Eskimo dog—and half wolf. Many dogs who are part wolf never become tame. They never learn to trust people—or obey them either. Balto was different. He was a gentle dog who obeyed orders quickly. He also knew how to think for himself.

Usually Gunnar Kasson guided the dogs. He told them where to go. Now he couldn't even see his hand in front of his face. So everything was up to Balto. The big black dog would have to find the trail by smell. Then he'd have to stay on it no matter what happened.

Gunnar Kasson climbed onto the back of the sled. He cracked his whip in the air. "*Mush!*" he cried. "*Move out!*"

The first part of the trail to Nome led across the sea ice. This ice wasn't anything like ice on a small pond or lake. It seemed much more *alive*. And no wonder. The water *under* the ice was moving up and down because of the storm. So the ice was moving up and down too. Up and down, up and down it went, like a roller coaster.

In some places the ice was smooth—as smooth and slippery as glass. Dogs are usually sure-footed. But they slipped and skidded across this ice. So did the sled.

And sometimes the ice came to sharp points—points that dug deep into the dogs' paws.

Worst of all were the places where the ice was bumpy—so bumpy that the sled turned over again and again. Each time it turned over the other dogs began to bark and snap at each other. But Balto always stood quietly while Kasson set the sled upright again. Balto was calm, so the other dogs grew calmer too.

The team had been moving across the ice for hours.

Suddenly there was a loud *cracking* sound—like a gun going off. Kasson knew that sound. It was the sound of ice breaking. Somewhere not far ahead the ice had split apart. If the team kept going straight they would run right into the freezing water—and drown.

Balto heard the ice crack too. He slowed for a moment. Then he turned left. He headed straight out to sea. He went for a long time. Then he turned right once more.

Balto was leading the team *around* the icy water. Finally he gave a sharp bark and turned north. He had found the trail to Nome again.

Soon the trail left the sea ice. From now on it was over land. Things should have been easier. They weren't. The snow was falling thick and fast. In some places the wind swept most of it off the trail. But in other places the snow drifts came up almost over the dogs' heads. And the wind was blowing harder and harder. It sent bits of icy snow straight into Kasson's eyes. "I might as well have been blind," he said. "I couldn't even *guess* where we were."

And the dogs were so tired! Again and again they tried to stop. They wanted to lie down and go to sleep in the snow. Balto was just as tired. But he would not stop. He kept on pulling—and the other dogs had to follow behind.

Now something else began to worry Gunnar Kasson. They had been traveling for about 14 hours. Surely they should have reached the town of Safety in 14 hours. Kasson went on for another hour. Then he knew. Somehow they had missed the town in the storm. They must have passed right by the new dog team!

Kasson knew they couldn't stop and wait for the storm to die down. He and the dogs would freeze if they did. They couldn't go back to Bluff either. They had come too far. There was only one thing to do now. Pray . . . and push on to Nome.

Later Gunnar Kasson said he couldn't remember those last miles very well. Each one was a nightmare of howling wind and swirling snow and bitter cold. But somehow—with Balto leading slowly and steadily—they made it! At 5:30 in the morning, February 2, 1925—after 20 hours on the trail—the team limped into Nome!

The whole town was waiting for the medicine! They gathered around Gunnar Kasson. They shook his hand and pounded him on the back. "How can we ever thank you?" one woman cried.

Gunnar Kasson shook his head. Then he sank to his knees beside Balto. He began to pull long splinters of ice from the dog's paws. "Balto, what a dog," he said. "I've been in Alaska for 20 years and this was the toughest trip I've ever made. But Balto, *he* brought us through."

Many newspaper and magazine stories were written about Balto. His picture was printed on postcards and in books. And today, on a grassy hill in New York City's Central Park, there is a life-sized statue of Balto—the dog who saved Nome.

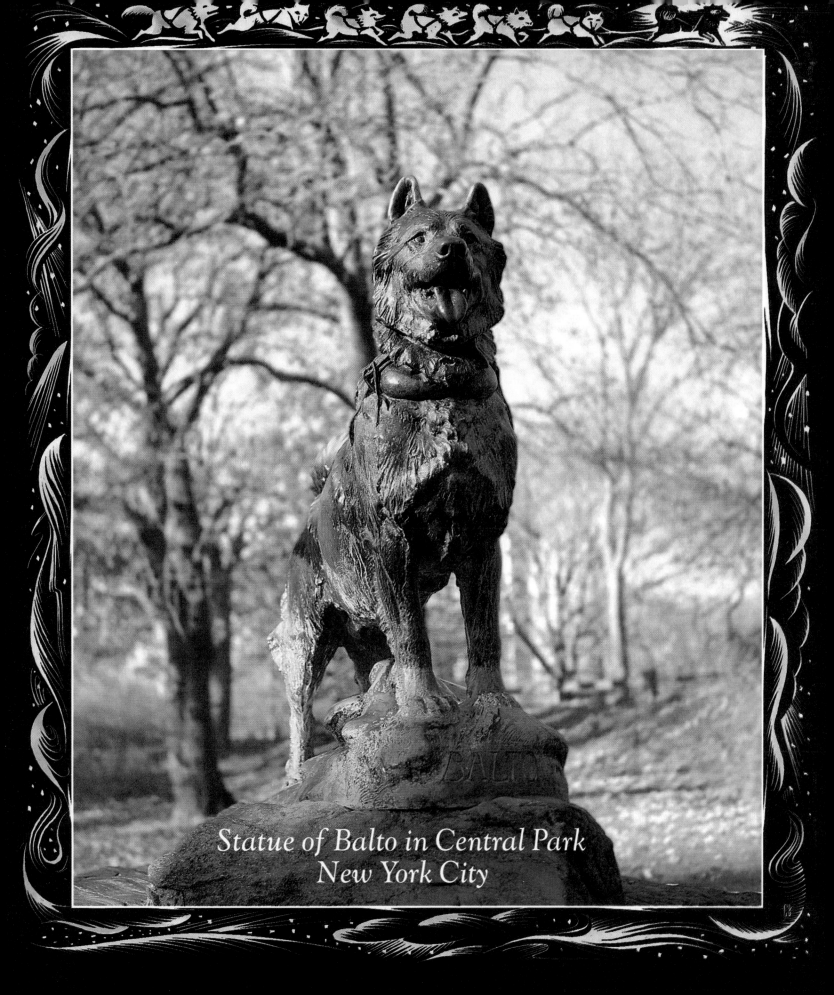

Statue of Balto in Central Park
New York City

Photos by JUSTIN SUTCLIFFE

Puppygarten Star

Meet Rosie, an
awesome dog with a
great job! Rosie visits
people. It's her job
to help cheer them up.

Paws down, Rosie is a great visiting dog. She is a Tibetan terrier, good-natured and friendly. Those traits gave her a head start. School gave her the skills.

Puppygarten

Rosie's owner, Stephanie Calmenson, took her goofy, playful puppy to kindergarten. There a teacher taught Rosie to "sit," "stay," "lie down" and "come" on command.

Later, Rosie joined a special visiting dog program for advanced training.

Love Knots

Kids Rosie visits like to care for her. This boy, who is blind, enjoys brushing Rosie's fur.

Lap Dog

Rosie makes friends wherever she goes. Thomas likes Rosie, so he doesn't mind her getting comfortable on his lap.

Think About Reading

1. Why did the people in Nome need medicine?

2. Why did Kasson and his dog team have to go all the way to Nome?

3. What do you think made Balto keep going?

4. Do you think Balto was a good lead dog? Why or why not?

5. The story ends with one photograph. Why do you think photographs aren't used in the rest of the story?

Write a Sign

Think about the statue of Balto. What do you think people should know about Balto when they look at that statue? Write a sign to go under Balto's statue.

Literature Circle

How did Balto help people? How does Rosie help people? Do you think the dogs could have traded places? Why or why not? Share your ideas with the rest of your group.

Author
Margaret Davidson

For Margaret Davidson, the most interesting stories are true. That's why most of her books are nonfiction. They tell the true stories of real people and real animals. Davidson has had several different jobs. Now she knows that writing books for young readers is what she likes most.

More Books by Margaret Davidson

- *Nine True Dolphin Stories*
- *Five True Horse Stories*
- *Helen Keller's Teacher*

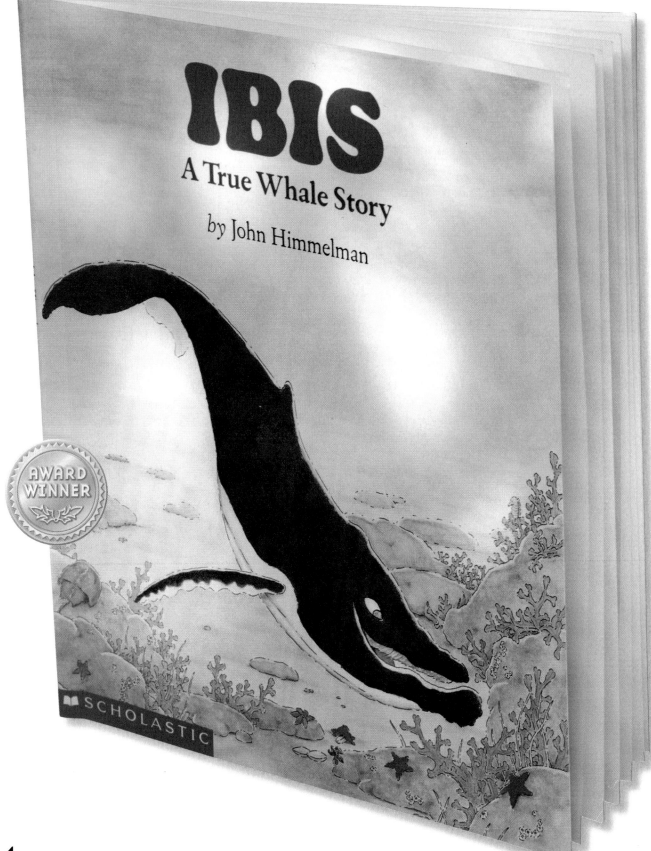

IBIS

A True Whale Story

by John Himmelman

AWARD WINNER

SCHOLASTIC

Deep in a bay,

off the coast of an old fishing village,

lived a pod of humpback whales.

One of the whales
was a little calf named Ibis.
Ibis was curious about everything in the ocean.

One day she and her friend Blizzard
went out swimming. They saw many kinds of fish.
The most interesting were the starfish.
Ibis liked to look at them.
There was something about their shape
that made her feel good.

As Ibis and Blizzard were drifting over a reef
they heard a strange humming noise.
The two calves looked up to see something
large and dark pass overhead.
It was as big as a whale,
but it wasn't a whale.

The calves were frightened.
They had never seen a boat before.
They swam back to their mothers.

The next day, Ibis went back to the reef.

It wasn't long before another boat came along.

Again, Ibis was scared. But she was curious, too.

She forced herself to swim to the surface.

In the cool, hazy air, she saw several faces
watching her. They didn't look scary.
In fact, they looked very friendly.
Ibis liked them.

In the months that followed, Ibis and her friends
lost their fear of boats. Boats came in many sizes
and shapes, and the people in them always seemed
to enjoy seeing the little whales.

As Ibis grew up, she learned more about the sea.

She knew what kinds of sharks to avoid,

what food was the tastiest,

and, best of all, where to find the most dazzling starfish.

Ibis never got tired of looking at starfish.

People and their boats became a part of her life.
Whenever a boat passed overhead, she swam to the top
to say hello.

One evening, Ibis and Blizzard saw a school of fish
swimming around the bottom of a ship.
Maybe there was something good up there to eat.
They went to find out.

Suddenly Ibis was caught in a fishing net!
She fought to get free. But the more she struggled,
the more tangled up she became.

Finally she broke loose, but part of the net
was caught in her mouth and wrapped around her tail.

Blizzard swam off to find help.

Ibis was confused and hurt.
She wanted to get away, far from people
and their boats and nets.
Slowly and painfully she made her way
toward the deep ocean.

Many weeks passed, and Ibis grew very ill.
The net in her mouth made it hard for her to eat.
And every time she went to the surface for air,
the net cut into her tail. But if she didn't
get air every half hour, she would die.

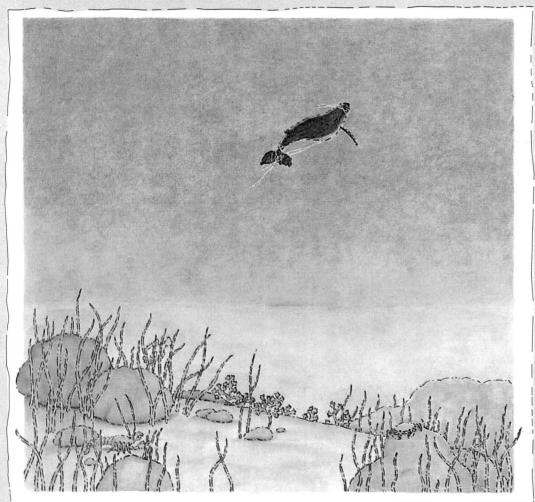

Winter was coming, and it was time for the whales
to move to warmer waters.
But Ibis felt too weak to make the long journey.

Instead she turned back toward the coast.
It was so hard for her to swim,
she could barely keep moving.
Ibis was about to give up.
Then she saw a familiar shape.
It was Blizzard!

Blizzard saw that Ibis needed help.
Gently Blizzard pushed her to the surface
so she could breathe.

Suddenly the water was filled with the sounds
of boat engines.
The whales saw two small rafts
and a boat circling them.

Blizzard and Ibis tried to get away fast.
But Ibis wasn't quick enough.
The boats rushed toward her before she could dive.

The people in the boats began to attach large floats
to the pieces of net that were hurting Ibis.
Blizzard stayed nearby,
circling the boats nervously.

Because of the floats, Ibis could not dive.
She began to panic,
but she did not have the strength to fight.
When the boats came in closer,
a person reached into the water.

Ibis stared at the person's hand.
The hand reminded her of something—
something she loved very much.
She began to feel better.

Soon many hands dipped into the water.
Ibis felt them tugging at the lines of the net.
Moments later the lines fell away, and she was free!

Ibis blew a big spout from her blowhole
as if to say, "Thank you! Thank you!"
Then she dived deep into the water.
For the first time in many weeks, she felt no pain.
She felt wonderful!

Blizzard joined her.

Then the two whales popped back to the surface

for one more look.

The people were waving their starfish-shaped hands.

Ibis knew the hands had helped her,

and that the people were still her friends.

Soon Blizzard and Ibis were leaping and diving
with the other whales, far away in the warm waters
where they would spend the winter together.

Working With

Dr. Carole Carlson and David Mattila work at the Center for Coastal Studies in Provincetown, Massachusetts. They are just two of the many people who work there.

Some work inside, at desks. Others work outside, on boats. They are all there for one reason. They are all trying to find out about the animals in the ocean, especially about whales.

Whales

Some people from the center go out to sea to gather information. Once the information is gathered, it is put into a computer. It can then be shared with people in other parts of the country.

People who use this information will know how whales live, move, and eat. The people will then be able to help whales if they get into trouble.

Ibis was one of the whales Carlson, Mattila, and their team helped. She was the first whale ever saved that was tangled in a fishing net.

233

Think About Reading

Think about *Ibis: A True Whale Story.* Finish each sentence in the story map. Do your work on another sheet of paper. Draw a picture to go with each sentence.

In the beginning,_____
_____.

↓

In the middle,_____
_____.

↓

In the end,_____
_____.

Write a Journal Entry

Imagine you were one of the people who helped Ibis. Write a journal entry to tell about that day. Tell about seeing the whale. Also tell what you and the other people on the boat did to help the whale.

Literature Circle

The team of scientists in "Working With Whales" helped save Ibis. Why do you think they—and other people like them—want to help whales? Talk about your ideas.

Author
John Himmelman

One morning, John Himmelman was on the deck of a ship near Provincetown, Massachusetts. A whale swam right over to the ship. A scientist on board told Himmelman that, just one year before, this same whale had been rescued from a net. That whale was the real Ibis! Seeing her close up made Himmelman want to write about Ibis.

More Books by
John Himmelman

- *The Animal Rescue Club*
- *Lights Out!*
- *Wanted: Perfect Parents*

235

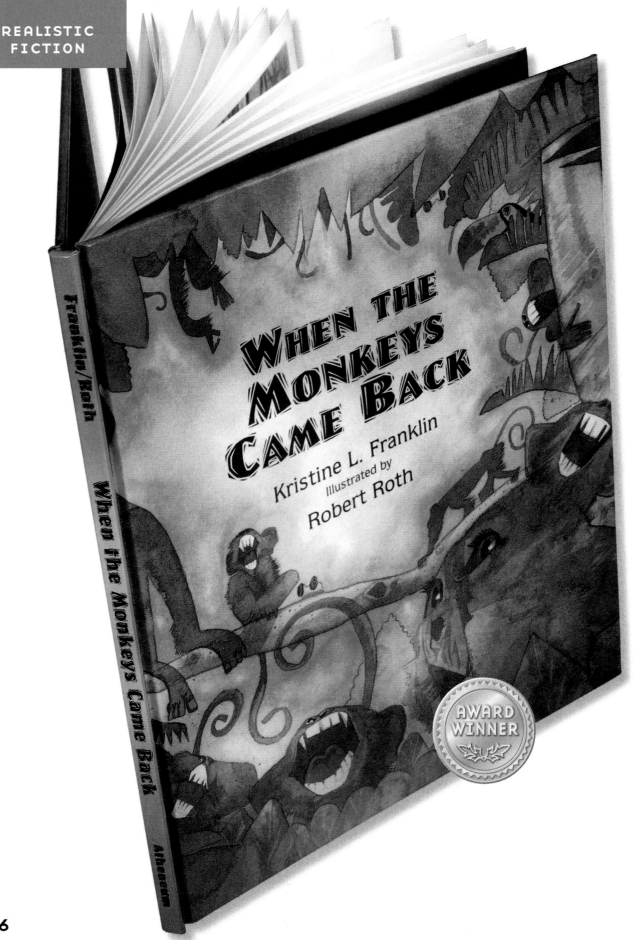

When the
Monkeys
Came Back

Kristine L. Franklin

Illustrated by
Robert Roth

AWARD
WINNER

When Doña Marta was a very little girl, the valley was a peaceful place. Children giggled as they chased each other between rows of tall corn. Fathers whistled as they dug in the gardens. Mothers hummed softly as they wrapped black beans and cornmeal in banana leaves to cook.

237

There was one old road in the valley, but it was an ox-cart road, an open place for meeting friends or cousins, a nice place for walking, a sunny place for catching lizards. There weren't any cars at all. The valley was a quiet place, except when the monkeys called.

Every morning and every evening for as long as anyone could remember, the monkeys announced the changing of night into day, the changing of day into night. At dawn they would howl and bark to one another, and the noise they made was like thunder in the trees. At dusk they would hoot and scream, and each leaf and each blade of grass would tremble from the sound.

One day a car chugged and sputtered up the old road. After that more cars came, not many at first, for the road was an ox road, not a car road. Marta was afraid of the cars. The sound and smell made her hide behind her mother's skirt. More and more cars came, and trucks, and more noise. Before long it wasn't safe to walk down the middle of the road, to stand and talk, to chase the quick lizards.

Still the monkeys shouted from the trees, drowning out all the new noises for a few moments each day, hooting to one another as they always had, waking up the world in the morning, calling the workers home from the fields at night.

The rains came and went and Marta's dress grew too short, and one day some men from the city came to Marta's house. They offered her father a lot of money, enough to buy six cows *and* a brand new dress for Marta, and asked to cut down some trees on the side of the mountain. Marta's father agreed and from that day on, the forest began to disappear.

At first it was just a few trees. The lumbermen cut down only the biggest trees, the ones with the hanging vines. The monkeys didn't seem to mind. They howled and barked and scolded just as before. But five years later, when there were only twenty-four trees left in the forest, the monkeys went away.

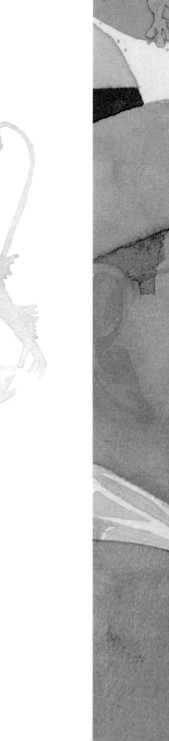

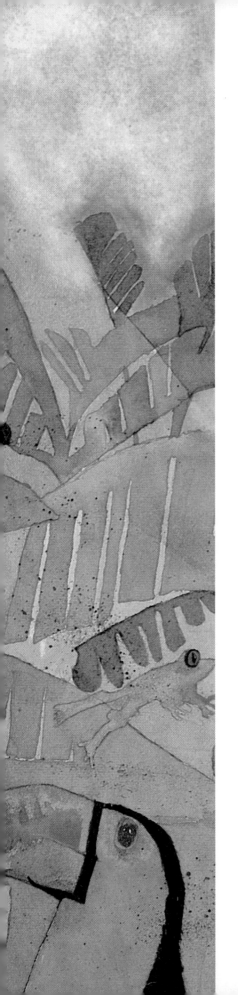

Marta didn't know where the monkeys went. One night, just as the sun slipped behind the hills, the monkeys shrieked and hooted and cried, louder than ever before. Some said it was because of the full moon. Others said the rainy season was near. But the next morning the valley was as silent as a stone.

Over the next several years the last of the trees was cut down. What had once been a forest was now covered with stumps and tangled brush. There were a few birds but no monkeys.

Most people forgot about the monkeys. They had roosters to wake them up in the morning, lamps to work by at night. But Marta didn't forget.

When she was fifteen years old Marta married Emilio. Emilio worked for Marta's father and when her father died, he left his farm to Marta and Emilio.

"You have a lot of land now," said Marta one day. "I would like to have some of it for myself." Emilio laughed out loud, because in those days, women did not own land.

"Soon we will have a family to feed," said Emilio. "After I plant corn and beans and squash, there will be nothing left over to give you. The rest of the land belongs to the cows."

"What about the land on the side of the mountain?" asked Marta. "There are too many stumps for a garden. And it is too steep for cows."

"That's true," agreed Emilio, and though it went against the custom, he gave the land on the side of the mountain to Marta.

"What are you going to do with your land?" asked Emilio.

"I'm going to bring back the forest," said Marta, and that is what she did.

Marta planted trees from the foot of the mountain to as far up as she could climb. When the sun baked the ground in the dry season, she hauled buckets of water to the trees. When the hard rains washed the little trees from the soil, she gently replanted them.

Year after year, Marta took care of the trees. In the next fifteen years she gave birth to eleven children. Each child learned to plant and tend trees. Year after year, Marta's children grew tall and so did the trees.

"Coffee grows well on a mountain," Emilio would tease. "Maybe you could plant coffee on your land." But Marta didn't listen. She didn't change her mind, and the forest came back.

Many more years passed. The trees grew higher and higher. Marta's children grew up and had children of their own. Emilio died and left the farm to Marta and her sons.

One day old Doña Marta took a walk along the road in the warm sunshine. The children greeted her as she passed.

"Good morning, Tree Lady," they said.

"Good morning," answered Doña Marta with a wink and an old, old smile. She leaned on her stick and stared across the valley.

Her trees touched the sky. Thick vines wrapped around their trunks. Birds of every color filled their branches. Now, wherever they dropped their seeds, new trees would grow. The valley was bright with squash and corn and beans, but the side of the mountain was a deep, dark green, forest green. Doña Marta's work was finished.

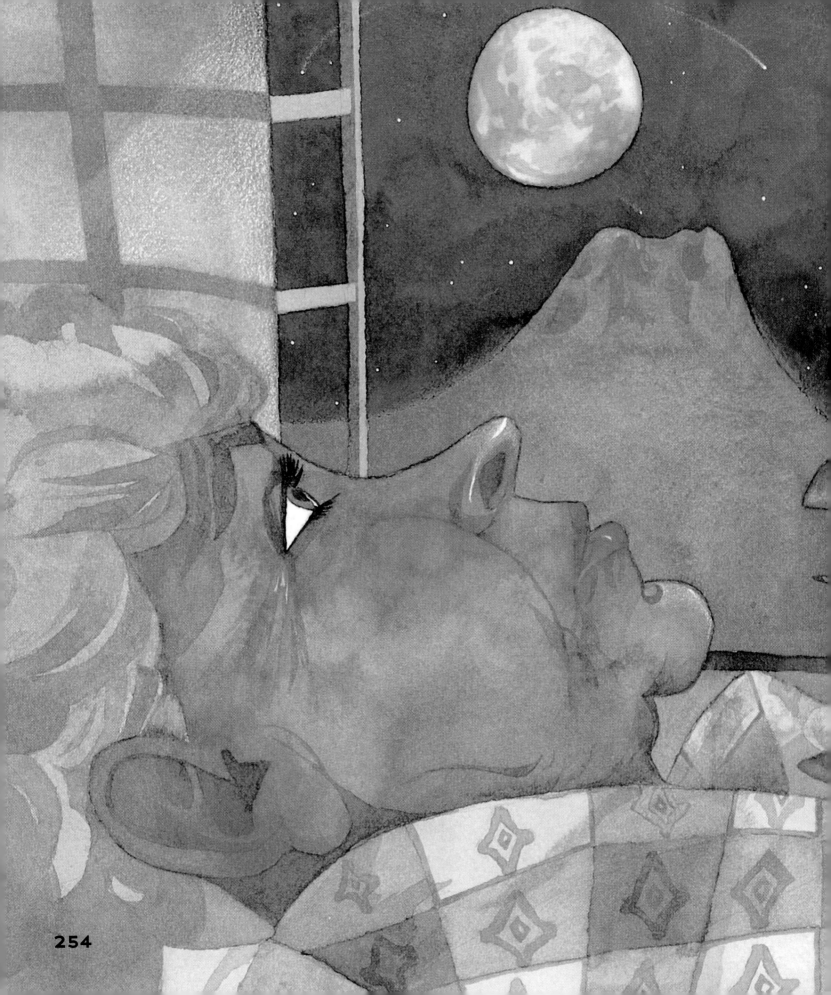

One night, Doña Marta couldn't sleep. As she lay in her bed she listened to the sounds of insects, the twittering of the night birds. Out her little window she watched the stars trail across the black sky. She watched the moon shadows shift and change in her room. As dawn approached, she heard the roosters begin to crow. And then she heard another sound.

At first it sounded like the barking of dogs, but soon the barking turned into howling, the howling into shrieks, the shrieks into shouts, and every leaf and every blade of grass trembled with the sound. Doña Marta hobbled to the window and leaned out.

The dark air thundered with the sound of monkeys hooting, howling, screaming from the treetops, waking up the whole world once again. Doña Marta closed her eyes, smiled a wrinkled smile, and listened to the music she had missed for fifty-six long years.

Every morning now, old Doña Marta wakes up to the barking and scolding of the monkeys. Every evening she waits for them to gather in the trees to shriek and howl and say good night. For a few moments each morning and evening, the sound of the monkeys drowns out all the other sounds in the valley. For a few moments each day, it's as if nothing had ever changed.

MENTOR

Lisa Stevens

Zoo Curator

**Do you like to go to the ZOO?
Some people go EVERY DAY!**

please don't feed the zoo animals

AMERICAN ASSOC. OF ZOO KEEPERS

Lisa Stevens is a curator of mammals at the National Zoo in Washington, D.C. She is in charge of many keepers, who take care of a giant panda, two camels, and over fifty apes and monkeys.

Lisa Stevens also talks to many visitors at the zoo. She talks about the animals and about protecting them.

Questions

for Lisa Stevens

Here's how zoo curator Lisa Stevens works with her staff to care for animals.

Q **What do you do to help the animals every day?**

A I check to see that they are fed the right foods and are kept active. I make sure they have everything they need to be healthy.

Q **Have you had a problem recently with an animal?**

A Not too long ago, Hsing-Hsing, our panda, developed an eye infection. If we hadn't treated it, he could have gone blind. We found a way to put special eye drops in his eyes to fight the infection.

Q **How did you learn about the different animals?**

A I learned a lot of what I know on the job. I talked to all the keepers who worked with the animals before me. I looked at the records that are kept on each animal. I also went to the library and read as much as I could about the animals.

JR PM	PENSI& CHANG PM	PYGMY MARMOSETS PM
APPLE..... 1lb	APPLE 18oz	*1/8 CAN OF MARMOSET DIET
ORANGES ... 1lb	ORANGES .. 18oz	*1/8 APPLE
BANANAS.... 1lb	BANANAS .. 18oz	*1/8 ORANGE
VEG DU JOUR .. 6oz	VEG DU JOUR .. 8oz	*1/8 BANANA
		*4 GRAPES
EGG(WED) 1	EGG(WED) 2	*15 MEALWORMS
MEAT(SAT) ... 8oz	MEAT(SAT) ... 8oz	NOTES: _____
NOTES: _____	NOTES: _____	_____

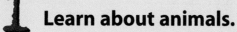

Lisa Stevens's Tips
for Helping Endangered Animals

1 Learn about animals.

2 Recycle. Don't pollute or waste water. If we save the earth, we help animals that need a place to live.

3 Support your local zoo.

THINK ABOUT READING

Think about *When the Monkeys Came Back.* Finish this story map. Do your work on another sheet of paper. Draw a picture to go with each sentence.

At first many monkeys live in the trees.

Then_____.

After five years, _____.

Then_____.

The trees grow and grow.

At last _____.

WRITE A SPEECH

The people in Doña Marta's valley are so happy that the monkeys have come back! They are planning a special party for her. The people will sing and dance and make speeches. If you could give a speech at the party, what would you say about Doña Marta and the monkeys? Write the short speech you would give.

LITERATURE CIRCLE

Both Doña Marta and Lisa Stevens know a lot about monkeys. Suppose that they meet. What do you think they would tell each other about themselves?

AUTHOR
KRISTINE L. FRANKLIN

When Kristine L. Franklin was in the second grade, she went to a library for the first time and discovered books. She can remember the look and smell of those library books. Now Franklin is grown-up, and she's still in love with books. Besides reading books, she writes them. She thinks she has the most wonderful job in the world!

MORE BOOKS BY
KRISTINE L. FRANKLIN

- *Iguana Beach*
- *The Old, Old Man and the Very Little Boy*
- *The Shepherd Boy*

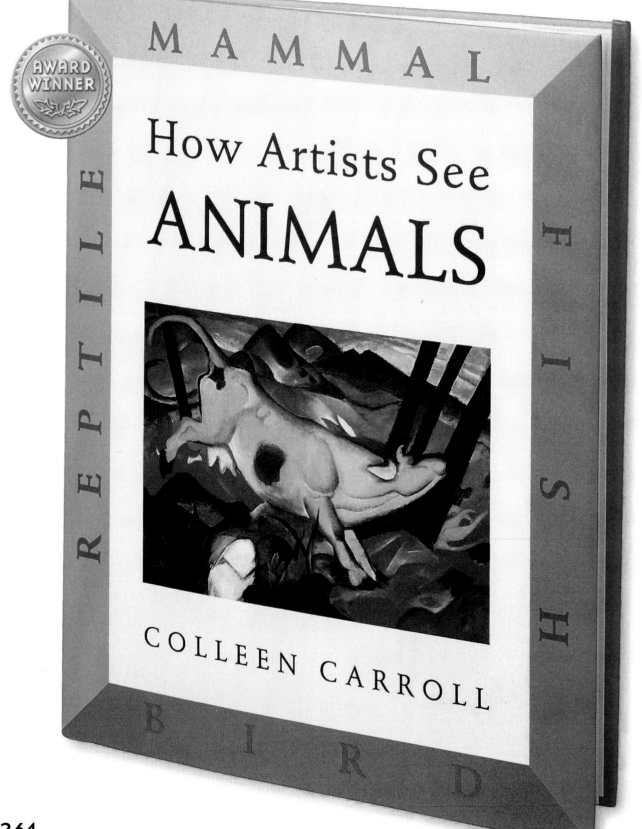

AWARD
WINNER

MAMMAL

REPTILE

FISH

BIRD

How Artists See
ANIMALS

COLLEEN CARROLL

264

THE GOLDFISH BOWL

by Henri Matisse

You've probably seen these fish before. Well, not these exact fish, but fish like them. They're goldfish, of course. You may even have your very own goldfish bowl at home or at school. These special goldfish swim in a bowl surrounded by vivid colors and bold patterns. Some of the patterns are made of shapes that look like fish. Point to all the fish-shaped objects you can find. Now look at the blurry patches of orange floating at the top of the bowl. What do you think they are?

GOLDFISH BOWL, II
by Roy Lichtenstein

Here's another bowl of goldfish made by a different artist. It has many things in common with the picture you just saw, but the artists have created two very different works of art. First, this artwork is a sculpture made from metal. The other is a painting. Second, these fish are darker and have heavy black outlines. What other similarities and differences can you find? Which fish look more real to you?

Sometimes artists get ideas by looking at the works of other artists whom they respect and admire. Then they add their own unique style to make the work new and original. Which style do you prefer?

THE FISH

by Alexander Calder

Artists often use materials in very clever ways. This sculpture
is made with lots of odds and ends, such as broken glass,
buttons, beads, and stones—the kinds of things that most
people would throw away. Some of the pieces were made
by hand, like the spiral object in the fish's tail. What other
unusual materials can you find? These bits and pieces help

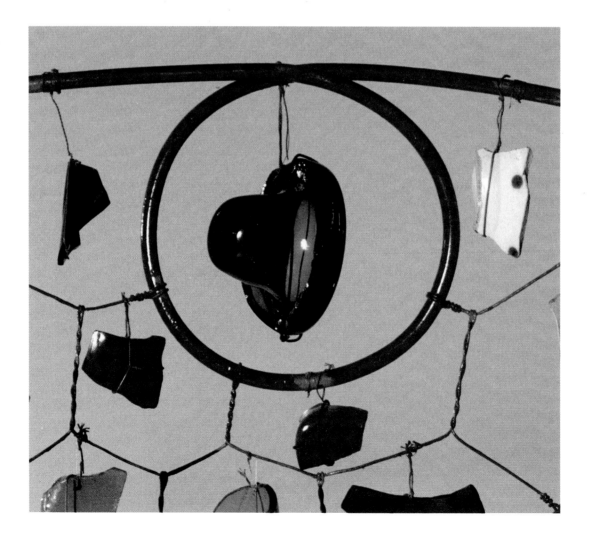

you to imagine the texture of a fish's scales. Are they smooth and slippery or rough and sharp? How is the round, green glass similar to a fish's eye?

This type of sculpture, called a mobile, hangs from the ceiling in a museum and seems to "swim" through the air. Imagine the fish swimming through the water with its mouth agape. Do you think it's hungry? How many tiny fish do you think it could swallow at once?

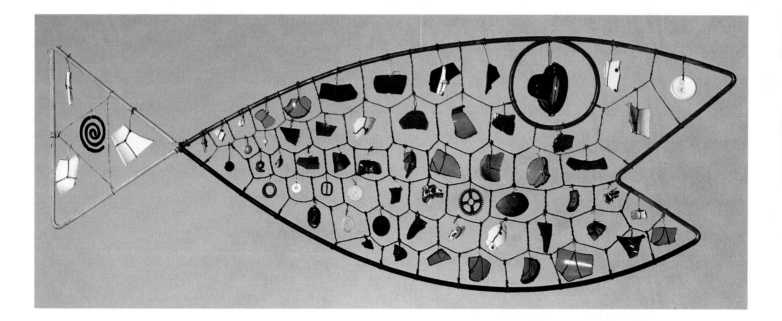

FISH MAGIC
by Paul Klee

There's something fishy going on here. The artist has
created a mysterious underwater world for a strange
school of fish. How many fish can you spot? Some of the
things in the picture you might expect to see in the water,
such as divers, flowers, and seaweed. But other things
don't seem to belong underwater. Can you find them?

Why do you think the artist named this painting *Fish Magic*?
With their bright colors against a black background, these
bizarre creatures seem to glow in the dark. Would you want
to swim in this eerie aquarium?

WHEATFIELD WITH CROWS

by Vincent Van Gogh

Where are the birds in this picture? If you noticed the black lines that look like flapping wings, you've found them. With just a few simple lines, the artist created a whole flock of crows. Have you ever drawn birds this way before?

Some of the larger birds seem to be very close, while
the smaller ones seem so far away that their shapes
blend into the sky. Perhaps they've flown a great distance
to reach the wheat field, or maybe they're flying away
to a different place. Do you think the crows are coming
or going? What sounds might you hear if you were
standing in this field?

BLACK BIRD OVER SNOW-COVERED RED HILLS

by Georgia O'Keeffe

Have you *ever* pretended to fly like a bird? Here's an artist who's shown the beauty of a bird in flight in a realistic way. If you could hitch a ride on the back of this sleek, painted blackbird, what would you see on the ground below?

This artist has used gently curving lines to make this graceful bird and to help you imagine what it must feel like to fly. The bird soars through a wide, open sky with extended wings. Move your finger over the lines of its body. Now trace these same lines through the air with your arms, as if you were a bird gliding over these snowy hills.

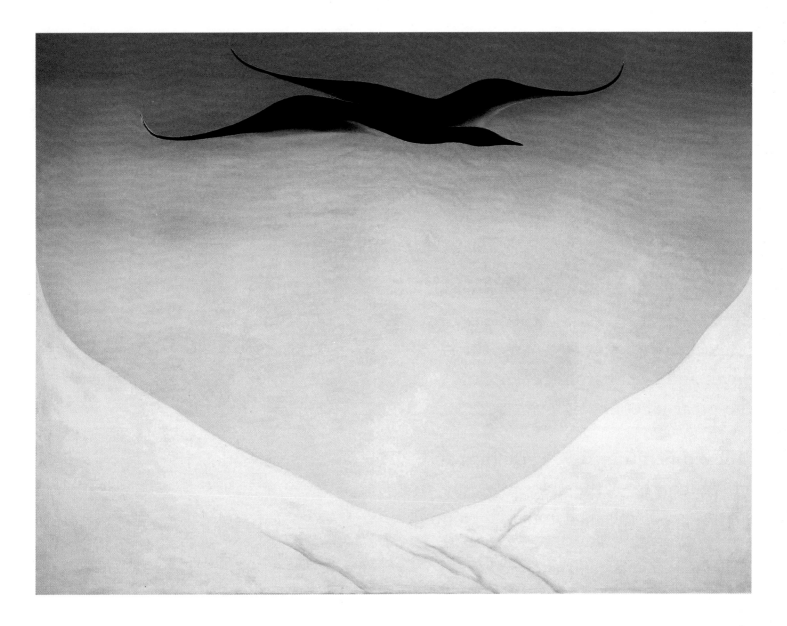

from *Colorín Colorado*

ANiMAL MESSENGERS

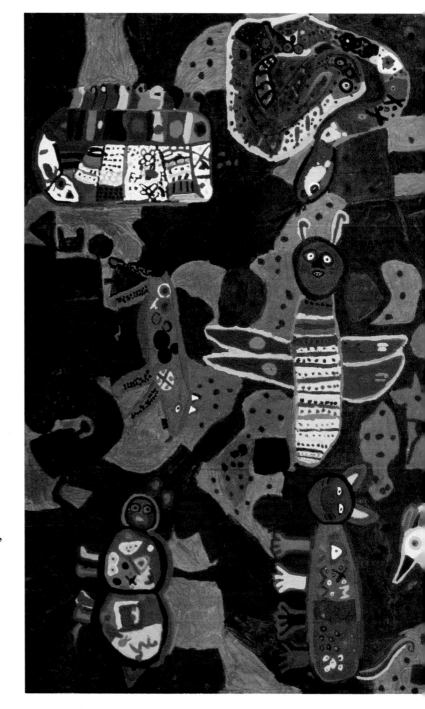

The artists who painted these animals are all children! These young painters live in Mexico. Read what they have to say about their work, their home in the jungle, and the many animals they see every day.

"The jungle is my home, the duck lives there and the dog; there are peacocks, wild turkeys, hens, turtle doves and even herons because of the great lagoon."

"I loved painting the *Xtacai* bird and the dragonfly; if the dragonfly enters the house, it means company's coming."

"They say that when the cicada goes way up in the tree, it won't rain for a long time."

276

Think About Reading

1. What two kinds of animals do the artists show?

2. Why does *The Fish* by Alexander Calder look hungry?

3. Look at *Wheatfield With Crows* and *Black Bird Over Snow-Covered Red Hills*. How are the paintings alike? How are they different?

4. Which of the six artworks do you like best? Why?

5. If you could meet one of these artists, which one would you choose? Why?

Write a Description

Choose your favorite picture in *How Artists See Animals.* Look at it carefully. Notice as many details as you can. Then write your own description of the artwork in that picture.

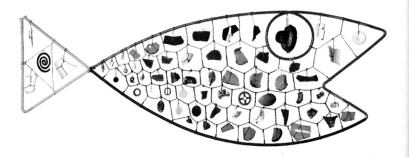

Literature Circle

The things shown in *Animal Messengers* are very special to the children who painted them. Do you think the things in *Fish Magic* are special to Paul Klee? What might they mean to him? Why do you think he painted those things?

AUTHOR
Colleen Carroll

Colleen Carroll has always been interested in art. When she taught sixth grade, she found out that many children are interested in art. Now Carroll writes books about artists and their work.

More Books by Colleen Carroll

- *How Artists See Families*
- *How Artists See the Weather*
- *How Artists See Work*

LEND A HAND

THEME
People can make
a difference in
their communities.

**The Little Painter
of Sabana Grande** **284**
by Patricia Maloney Markun

from **My Painted House,
My Friendly Chicken, and Me** **308**
by Maya Angelou

Fire Fighters **316**
by Robert Maass

MENTOR
Police Officer **Nadine Jojola** **340**

from **The Many Lives of
Benjamin Franklin** **346**
by Aliki

Yankee Doodle **356**

Follow the Drinking Gourd **362**
by Jeanette Winter

The Underground Railroad **390**
by Glennette Turner

Miss Spider's Tea Party **394**
by David Kirk

GLOSSARY **426**

www.scholastic.com

Visit the kids' area of
www.scholastic.com for the
latest news about your favorite
Scholastic books. You'll find sneak
previews of new books, interviews
with authors and illustrators, and
lots of other great stuff!

UNIT 6

Welcome to

LITERACY PLACE

Go to a Police Station

People can make a difference in their communities.

The Little Painter of Sabana Grande

by Patricia Maloney Markun · illustrated by Robert Casilla

AWARD
WINNER

284

High in the mountains of Panama lies the village of Sabana Grande. It is very small. Just seven houses of clay adobe stand alongside a brook in a grassy meadow. In the middle house lives the Espino family.

At dawn one cool purple morning, the rooster next door crowed. The Espinos woke up.

Papa went off to the meadow to milk the cow.

Mama stirred up the fire in the open-air kitchen and fried golden breakfast tortillas.

Fernando rolled up his straw sleeping mat and put it in the corner. He hurried to the kitchen to eat his tortilla right away.

This was an important day. At school Fernando had learned to draw colored pictures with crayons. Now school was out for dry-season vacation, and Fernando was going to paint for the first time.

His teacher, Señora Arias, had told him exactly how the country people of Panama made their paints. She said:

"Black from the charcoal of a burned tree stump.
Blue of certain berries that grow deep in the jungle.
Yellow from dried grasses in the meadow.
And red from the clay on the bottom of the brook."

It took him a long time to make the paints. Black was easy, because the burned stump of a big tree lay right next to the Espinos' adobe house.

But Fernando had to look before he found those certain berries deep in the jungle, to make the blue paint.

In the corner of the meadow he found a patch of very dry grass, and from that he made a large pot of yellow.

He wandered up and down alongside the brook, looking for clay. The fast-flowing water was too deep for him to reach down to the bottom. At last he came to a bend in the brook where the water was shallow. He reached down and dug up a fistful of clay. It was red, just the way Señora Arias had said.

Now his paints were stirred up and waiting—black, blue, yellow, and red, in four bowls. Next he got out the three paintbrushes his teacher had given him—one very small, one medium-sized, and one especially large.

I'm ready to paint pictures, Fernando said to himself. He picked up the small brush and dipped it into the pot of red. Then he had a terrible thought.

He had nothing to paint a picture on! An artist needs paper.

He looked in both rooms of the house. He could find no paper at all.

He ran from house to house asking everyone in Sabana Grande for paper to paint on. None of the neighbors had any. Not a scrap.

Fernando was sad. After all his work he wouldn't be able to paint pictures—the colored pictures he could almost see, he wanted to make them so badly. Paints and brushes weren't enough. He needed paper, too.

291

His fingers itched to draw something—anything. He put down the paintbrush and went over to the mud by the brook. He picked up a stick and drew in the wet dirt, the way he had ever since he was a very little boy.

The big rooster who woke him every morning came out of the chicken yard next door. Fernando looked at him and drew the shape of a rooster. He sighed. He couldn't use his new red and yellow paints to make a bright rooster. He couldn't make the rooster's comb red. He could only scratch out a mud-colored rooster. It wasn't the same as painting would be. It didn't have any color.

Fernando looked around at the adobe houses of his village. Suddenly he got an idea. Adobe was smooth and white—almost like paper. Why couldn't he paint on the outside of his family's adobe house?

"No!" Papa said. "Who ever saw pictures on the outside of a house?"

"No!" Mama agreed. "What would the neighbors say?"

Fernando looked at his pots of paint and was very unhappy. He wanted to paint pictures more than anything else he could think of.

At last Papa said, "I can't stand to see my boy so miserable. All right, Fernando. Go ahead and paint on the house!"

Mama said, "Do your best, Fernando. Remember, the neighbors will have to look at your pictures for a very long time."

First Fernando made a tiny plan of the pictures he was going to paint, painting it with his smallest brush on one corner of the house.

"Your plan looks good to me, Fernando," Papa said. "If you can paint pictures small, you should be able to paint them big."

Fernando picked up his bigger brushes and started to paint a huge picture of the most beautiful tree in Panama, the flowering poinciana, on the left side of the front door. As he painted, he could look up and see the red flowers of a poinciana tree, just beginning its dry season, blooming on the mountainside.

The neighbors were very surprised.

Señora Endara called out, "Come and see what Fernando is doing!"

Señor Remon said, "Who ever saw a house with pictures on the outside?"

Pepita, the little girl next door, asked, "Does your mother know you're painting on your house?"

Fernando nodded and smiled and kept on painting. Now and then he would look up at the mountain to see the real poinciana. After a week its flowers faded and died. Fernando's tree grew bigger and brighter and redder.

On one branch he added a black toucan with a flat, yellow bill. On another branch a lazy, brown sloth hung by its three toes.

The neighbors brought out chairs. While Fernando worked, they drank coffee and watched him paint.

Next he painted the wall on the other side of the door. An imaginary vine with flat, green leaves and huge, purple blossoms crept up the wall.

Word spread about the little painter of Sabana Grande. Even people from Santa Marta, the village around the mountain, hiked into town to watch him paint. The purple vine now reached almost to the thatched roof.

One day Señora Arias came from the school in Santa Marta. Why was his teacher looking for him, Fernando wondered. It was still dry season, when there wasn't any school. It hadn't rained for a month.

"School's not starting yet," his teacher said. "I came to see your painted adobe house that everyone in Santa Marta is talking about. Fernando, you did very well with those paintbrushes. I like it!"

She turned to the neighbors. "Don't you?"

"We certainly do!" the neighbors agreed.

They poured some coffee for the visiting teacher.

"Fernando, will you paint pictures on my house?" asked Señora Alfaro.

"And mine, too?" asked Señor Remon.

Fernando nodded yes, but he kept on painting.

For fun he added a black, white-faced monkey looking down at the people through purple flowers.

Next to the door he painted a big red-and-yellow rooster, flopping its red comb as it crowed a loud "cock-a-doodle-doo!"

Above the door he painted the words CASA FAMILIA
ESPINO, so people would know that this was the home
of the Espino family.

Now his pictures were finished. Fernando sat down with his teacher and the neighbors. Everyone said kind words about his paintings.

Fernando said nothing. He just smiled and thought to himself, There are still six adobe houses left to paint in Sabana Grande.

from My Painted House, My Friendly Chicken, and Me

by Maya Angelou

photographs by Margaret Courtney-Clarke

Hello Stranger-friend.

I am Thandi, an Ndebele girl in South Africa.

All Ndebele women paint their houses, and I want you to know, stranger-friend, no one's house is as good as my mother's. She has started to teach me to paint good, very good designs.

When I am taller, I shall have a house so good people will stop in front of my walls and smile, and even laugh out loud.

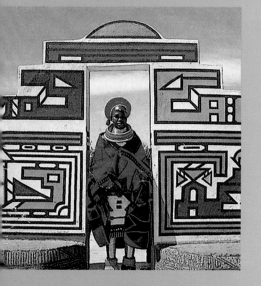

You have to
have strong
eyes to paint
good, and
your hand
must not
shake like a
leaf on a tree,
for you must
fill a chicken's
feather with
paint and
draw a line as
straight as a
spear.

You must have the

pattern inside your head,

even before you dip the

feather into the paint.

Your hand must be steady to make the patterns sharp,

and your legs must be strong, because sometimes the walls are high.

Think About Reading

Think about *The Little Painter of Sabana Grande*. Answer each question in the story map. Do your work on another sheet of paper. Draw a picture to go with each part of the story.

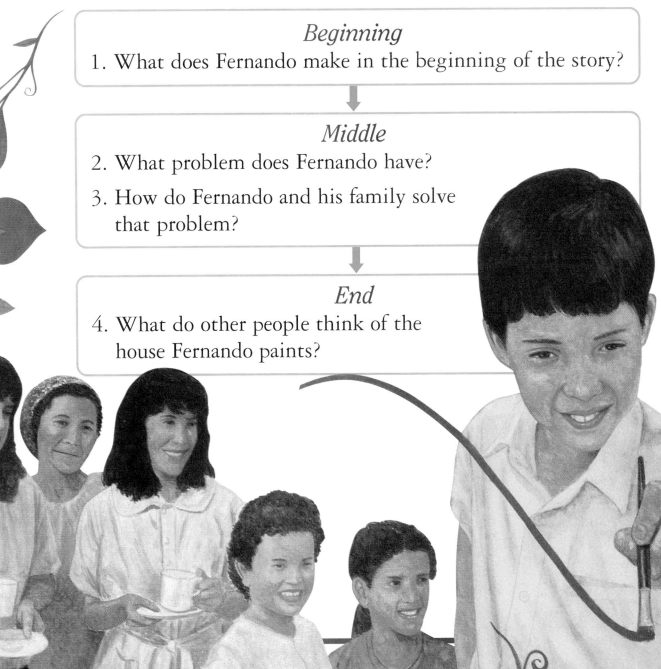

Beginning
1. What does Fernando make in the beginning of the story?

Middle
2. What problem does Fernando have?
3. How do Fernando and his family solve that problem?

End
4. What do other people think of the house Fernando paints?

Write a Description

What if you could visit Sabana Grande after a year had passed? How do you think the village would look? Write a description of Fernando's village.

Literature Circle

The Little Painter of Sabana Grande takes place in the mountains. How is this setting important to the story? How would the story be different if it took place near the beach? Talk about your ideas.

Illustrator
Robert Casilla

Illustrating *The Little Painter of Sabana Grande* was a treat for Robert Casilla. Like Fernando, Casilla loved to paint when he was young. Now he is a grown-up man, and he still loves to paint. Casilla also liked showing the village of Sabana Grande. He said it reminds him of Puerto Rico where he lived as a child.

More Books Illustrated by
Robert Casilla

- *Jalapeño Bagels*
- *A Picture Book of Jackie Robinson*
- *The Train to Lulu's*

AWARD
WINNER

What do fire fighters do?

They have many different jobs. Their most important job is fighting fires to save lives and property. They learn this job by going to school. They are taught by experienced fire fighters.

To be a fire fighter, one of the first things to learn is how to use ladders for climbing.

Fire fighters also learn how to use ropes. They use ropes the way mountain climbers do. With a rope, fire fighters can lower themselves down a wall.

Fire fighters in training learn all about the hoses they use to fight fires. They must practice the correct way to aim the nozzle. A fire hose shoots out water with great force. It takes skill to make sure the water goes where it is supposed to go.

The hoses are attached to fire hydrants and then to the *pumper truck.* The pumper truck pumps the water from the hydrants into the hoses the fire fighters use. These hoses are called *lines.* Controlling the amount of water that comes out of the lines is an important job. Fire fighters must learn to read the gauges on the pumper truck to know when to pump more or less water into the lines. It is a job that takes lots of practice.

There are many special tools the fire fighters must learn to use. One of these tools is called the "jaws of life." It is a very powerful tool that can cut through metal. It can also be used to pry things open. When people are stuck in cars or buildings, this tool can help get them out.

There are also simple tools a fire fighter needs. One of the most important is an ax. Fire fighters often need it to break through walls, ceilings, doors, and windows during a fire.

All fire fighters wear heavy coats and gloves when fighting fires. They also wear an unusual leather helmet. It protects them from water and from things that might fall from burning buildings.

A flashlight and a doorstop come in very handy, too. They are used so often that fire fighters sometimes carry them on their helmets.

Fire fighters also wear special gear. They need to
wear walkie-talkies to stay in touch with one another.
They wear heat-resistant clothing because the fire is
very hot. Often a fire fighter must carry a tank of air
to breathe when there is a lot of smoke.

Some fire fighters receive special training. They may be assigned to a *rescue unit*. The fire fighters in these units fight fires, but also need special skills. For example, some are trained in diving to fight ship or pier fires. Diving rescue units may also be called to help people who have boating or other water accidents.

Teamwork is a very important part of learning to be a fire fighter. Everyone must work together to save lives and put out fires. Fire fighters at school march together to practice being part of a team.

After several weeks the fire fighters' basic training is over. All fire fighters must pass a test on what they have learned. Then the fire fighters graduate.

The new graduates are assigned to work with experienced fire fighters at a fire station.

Here they will put their training into practice, and learn even more from the experienced fire fighters. There are many more jobs to learn at the fire station.

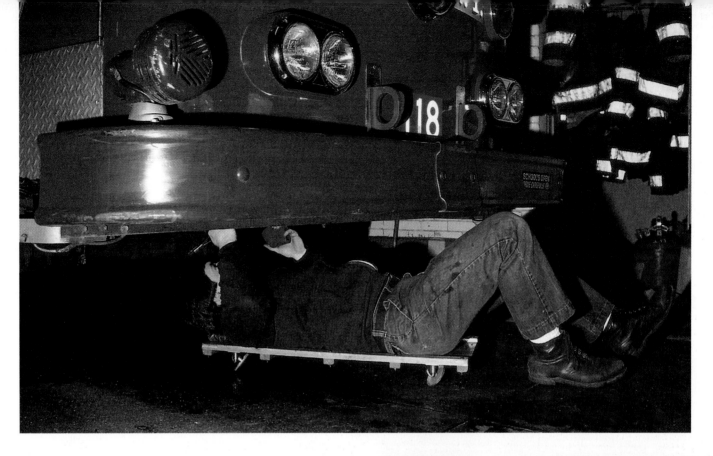

All of the equipment the fire fighters use must be kept in top shape. This means that repairs must be done as soon as anything goes wrong. New fire fighters learn to maintain and repair their equipment. Tools and trucks are checked and serviced every day, because everything must work perfectly when a fire or other emergency happens.

Fire fighters must also learn to check things outside of the fire station. They check all of the fire hydrants in the neighborhoods they serve, and inspect buildings for fire safety.

There are lots of other jobs around the fire station.

Fires can break out at any time, so fire fighters in many places must be at the fire station every day and every night. That means that the fire fighters on duty must cook their own meals.

When they go shopping for groceries, they must all go together. They take their walkie-talkies to keep in touch. If a fire starts somewhere, the fire fighters will have to leave the grocery store in a hurry.

There are often visitors at the fire station. School children sometimes come to learn about fire fighting and fire prevention.

When children can't come to the fire station, fire fighters visit schools. They talk to classes about fire prevention, and what to do in case of fire.

Fire fighters demonstrate how to *stop-drop-and-roll*. This is what you must do if your clothes catch on fire. **Stop:** Stop where you are. Don't run. **Drop:** Drop to the ground. **Roll:** Roll back and forth protecting your face with your hands to smother the flames.

When all of the work has been done at the fire station, there are other things to do. Some fire fighters may get a chance to read the paper. Some may exercise in order to keep in shape. There may be a dog to take care of, too.

Occasionally, fire fighters may even try to sleep. But no matter what fire fighters may be doing, they must always be ready. Because sooner or later, usually when no one is expecting it...the alarm will ring.

As soon as the alarm goes off, the fire fighters must put on their fire-fighting gear and get to their trucks as fast as they can. Many fire stations have poles to help fire fighters get downstairs. Poles are faster and safer than stairs. Everyone hurries. They know that the best way to control a fire is to get there as quickly as possible.

Each fire fighter has a special place on one of the trucks. As the engines pull out of the fire station, the fire fighters check the equipment they will need.

Some of the trucks need two drivers. One is in the front of the truck and one is at the back, or *tiller*. The one in the back handles the rear wheels of the longest fire trucks.

As soon as they arrive, the fire fighters jump off the trucks and go to work. Each fire fighter knows what to do.

A fire chief is on hand to direct the firefight.

Some of the fire fighters must *vent* the roof. That means they must break a hole in the roof to release fire and smoke trapped in the building. That will make it easier to fight the fire and rescue people inside.

332

Other fire fighters have attached the lines to pumper trucks. They begin to aim streams of water at the flames. Some must enter the building to fight the fire from inside.

Windows must sometimes be broken to let the smoke and heat out of the building. Fire fighters carry tanks of air on their backs so they can breathe pure air when the smoke is very thick.

The flames and smoke of the fire begin to disappear as the fire fighters gain control of it. After a while, the fire appears to be over. But the fire fighters' job is not over. They must carefully check the building to make sure that every bit of the fire is out.

Finally, the fire is completely out.

Struggling to put out a fire is exhausting work. Some of the fire fighters must rest before they put their equipment back into the trucks.

The fire-fighting team packs all of its tools and gear back into the trucks. Everything will be ready when the next fire occurs. The fire trucks return to the fire station. They back in so they will be ready to roll as soon as the alarm sounds again.

The fire fighters are happy to be back at the fire station. They are tired, but they are safe.

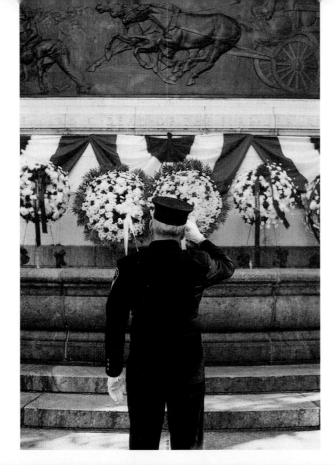

Fire fighting is very dangerous work. Sometimes fire fighters lose their lives in fires.

But the brave men and women who have died fighting fires are not forgotten. In almost every city and town, there is a monument to remember those who gave their lives trying to save others. At least once each year, fire fighters get together to remember.

In many places fire
fighters also get together
to take part in special
parades. Fire fighters
wash and shine all of their
trucks so they will look
their very best on parade
day. Then they get
dressed in fresh uniforms.

Fire fighters love
marching in parades with
music and flags.

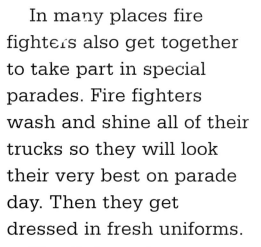

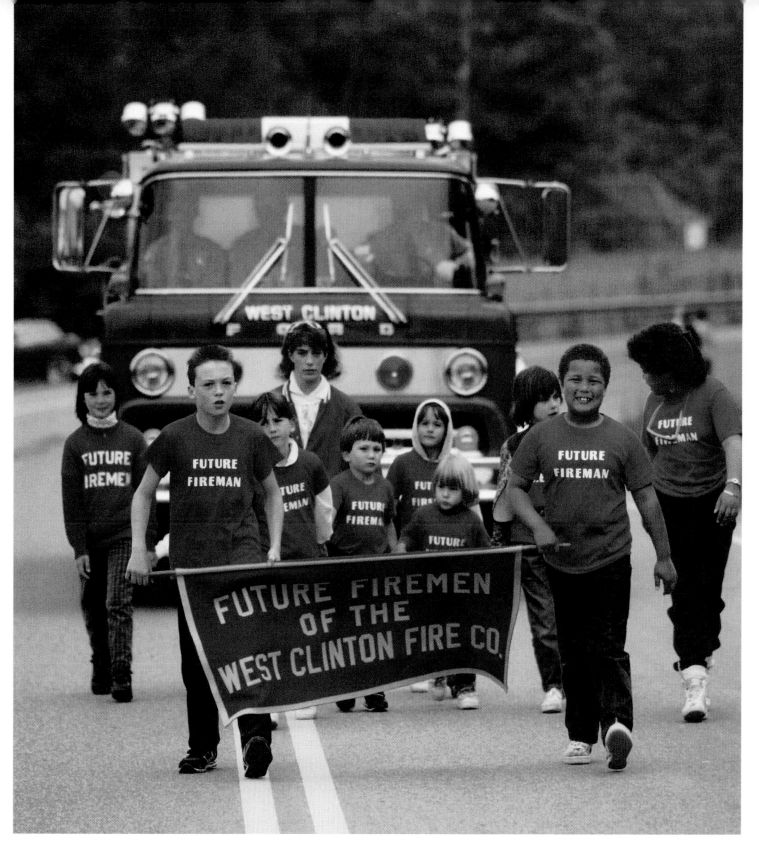

So do future fire fighters.

MENTOR

Nadine Jojola
Police Officer

**Do you think YOU can help the police?
You CAN—by keeping yourself safe!**

There are many kinds of workers who help people in their communities. When Nadine Jojola (ha-HOLE-ah) was a little girl, she wanted to be a teacher. Today she is a teacher, but not in a classroom.

Ms. Jojola is a police lieutenant in New Mexico. She teaches people in the pueblo of Isleta how to keep themselves safe in their community.

341

All About

Nadine Jojola

Here's how Police Lieutenant Nadine Jojola lends a hand in her community.

Lieutenant Jojola enjoys teaching people, especially children and the elderly. She tells them what is right and wrong. She says, "It's a big job to teach people about the law and how to keep their community safe."

A large river called the Rio Grande runs through the pueblo. Lieutenant Jojola teaches children how to keep themselves safe around the water. She tells them not to play in the river unless an adult is with them.

Lieutenant Jojola warns children about other dangers. She tells them never to go off with a stranger. She tells them how they can know if something is poison. She tells them they should never play with matches. She teaches children how to dial 911 in an emergency.

And, of course, she tells them that the police will always help with serious problems.

Nadine Jojola's
 Tips for Helping Police

1 If you see trouble, tell an adult what is wrong.

2 Learn about what can hurt you and how to keep yourself safe.

3 Ask the police for help with serious problems.

343

Think About Reading

1. What is the most important job fire fighters do?

2. What do the gauges on a pumper truck tell fire fighters?

3. Why do you think the "jaws of life" has that name?

4. Choose one photo in this selection. How does it help you understand the work fire fighters do?

5. How is a fire fighter's job like Nadine Jojola's job?

Write a List

What are the most important tips for being a good fire fighter? Write a list of at least four tips. If you want, draw pictures to go with your tips.

Literature Circle

Imagine that Nadine Jojola could visit the fire fighters in the selection. What do you think she would say to the fire fighters? What do you think the fire fighters would say to her?

Author
Robert Maass

Robert Maass started taking photographs when he was not much older than you are. He has always liked taking pictures that show both facts and feelings. He hopes that his photographs can help people understand each other better.

More Books by
Robert Maass

- *Tugboats*
- *When Autumn Comes*
- *Garden*

from

The Many Lives of Benjamin Franklin

By Aliki

Benjamin Franklin did so many amazing things that it seems as if he lived many lives. He opened a printing shop and printed his own newspaper. He lent out his many books and started the first free lending library in America. He started a police force, a fire department, and a hospital.

When he was forty-two, Benjamin Franklin gave up his print shop so he could spend all his time with his new ideas. He invented many useful things during this part of his life.

Ben started scientific experiments, and soon became a master.

He was the first to prove lightning was electricity.

One day, during a thunderstorm, he tried a dangerous experiment with a kite and a key, and found he was right.

He realized how to protect houses from lightning, and invented the lightning rod.

People put "Franklin Rods" up on their rooftops in America and in other countries, too.

He experimented in his garden and found better ways to grow crops.

He invented glasses called bifocals. He could see far, out of the top of the glasses, and near, out of the bottom.

He introduced Swiss barley, Chinese rhubarb, Newton apples, willow for baskets, and turnips to America.

He found out that black cloth keeps one warmer than white by laying pieces of cloth in the snow. After some time, the black cloth was warmed by the sun and sank into the snow. The white didn't.

Benjamin Franklin made many discoveries in his lifetime, but he refused money for them. He said his ideas belonged to everyone. He wrote them down and they were translated into many languages. He became the best known man in America.

Benjamin and his friends discussed ways to gain freedom for America.

More than anything, Benjamin hoped people would
listen to his most important idea—
freedom for his country.
For at that time, America was an English colony.
He—and others—did not want to be ruled by
England any longer.

He was sent to England to seek independence
for his country.
For eighteen long years, Benjamin stayed there
and worked for that goal.
In 1775, he returned to Philadelphia,
sad and disappointed.
His wife had died. War with England had begun,
and America was still not free.

Pennsylvania State House, now called Independence Hall, in 1776.

Benjamin Franklin, Thomas Jefferson, John Adams, John Hancock, and 52 others, signed the Declaration of Independence in Philadelphia on July 4, 1776.

Yet he persisted.

Benjamin Franklin and other great Americans
helped Thomas Jefferson write the Declaration of
Independence.

They were determined to be free.

They knew they would have to fight
a long, terrible war.

And fight they did.

General George Washington led many battles during the
Revolutionary War.

In France, he visited King Louis XVI and Queen Marie Antoinette. Though everyone wore fancy clothes and powdered wigs, Benjamin Franklin did not. Everyone was impressed with the inventor's plain clothes and simple ways.

But they needed more help.

Benjamin Franklin was old and weary when again

he sailed away.

This time he went to ask for aid from

the King of France.

Benjamin was greeted as a hero.

People in France knew about him and his inventions,

and they loved him.

Finally, the King agreed.

With his help, the war with England was won.

America was free at last.

In 1781 the war ended. The Liberty Bell in Independence Hall rang out.

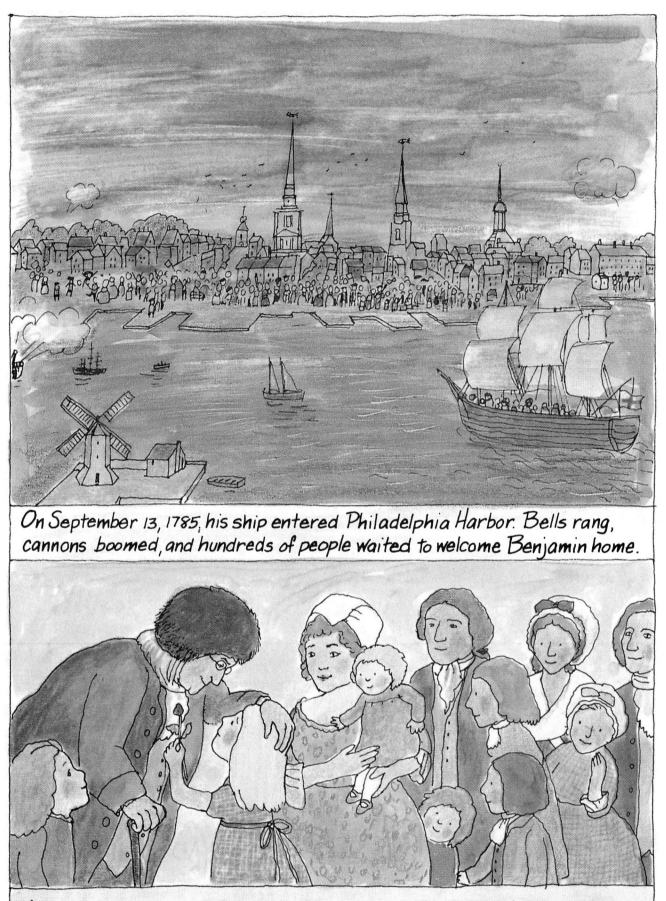

On September 13, 1785, his ship entered Philadelphia Harbor. Bells rang, cannons boomed, and hundreds of people waited to welcome Benjamin home.

He was reunited at last with his daughter Sally, her husband Richard Bache, and his grandchildren.

Benjamin Franklin had served abroad long enough.

He wanted to spend his last years at home.

When he finally returned from France, it was 1785.

He thought he had been forgotten.

But he had not been forgotten.

He was greeted with wild celebrations.

He saw his country still needed him.

He became the first governor of Pennsylvania and

helped write the Constitution of the United States.

Benjamin Franklin lived eighty-four years.

He left the world his inventions, his ideas,

his wisdom and his wit.

He lived his many lives for us all.

On September 17, 1787, Benjamin Franklin and the other great writers of the Constitution signed the document on which all laws of the United States are based.

YANKEE DOODLE

American Revolutionary War Song

Yankee Doodle went to town
A-riding on a pony,
Stuck a feather in his cap
And called it macaroni!

Yankee Doodle, keep it up,
Yankee Doodle dandy.
Mind the music and the step
And give the girls some candy.

Father and I went down to camp,
Along with Captain Goodwin.
And there we saw the men and boys
As thick as hasty pudding.

Yankee Doodle, keep it up,
Yankee Doodle dandy.
Mind the music and the step
And give the girls some candy.

And there was Captain Washington
Upon a slapping stallion,
A-giving orders to his men
I guess there was a million.

Yankee Doodle, keep it up,
Yankee Doodle dandy.
Mind the music and the step
And give the girls some candy.

Think About Reading

1. What are some things Benjamin Franklin did earlier in his life?

2. What is Benjamin Franklin's most important idea?

3. When Franklin returns from France, why does he think he has been forgotten?

4. Why do you think the author says that Benjamin Franklin "lived his many lives for us all"?

5. Look at the picture on page 352. Why do you think Benjamin Franklin wore simple clothes even though he was visiting the king and queen of France?

Write a Letter

Benjamin Franklin was still in France when the war with England ended. How do you think he felt when he heard the news? Maybe he wrote a letter to his daughter Sally, telling her about his feelings. Write a letter Franklin could have sent to Sally.

Literature Circle

Which of the amazing things that Benjamin Franklin did do you find the most interesting? Tell why.

Author
Aliki

Doesn't Aliki have more than one name? Yes—but she uses just her first name on the books she writes and illustrates. Before she got married, her name was Aliki Liacouras. Now her name is Aliki Brandenberg. Her husband, Franz Brandenberg, is a writer, too. Sometimes Aliki draws pictures for her husband's books.

More Books by Aliki

- *A Weed Is a Flower: The Life of George Washington Carver*
- *Mummies Made in Egypt*
- *Best Friends Together Again*

Long ago,
before the Civil War,
there was an old sailor called Peg Leg Joe
who did what he could to help free the slaves.

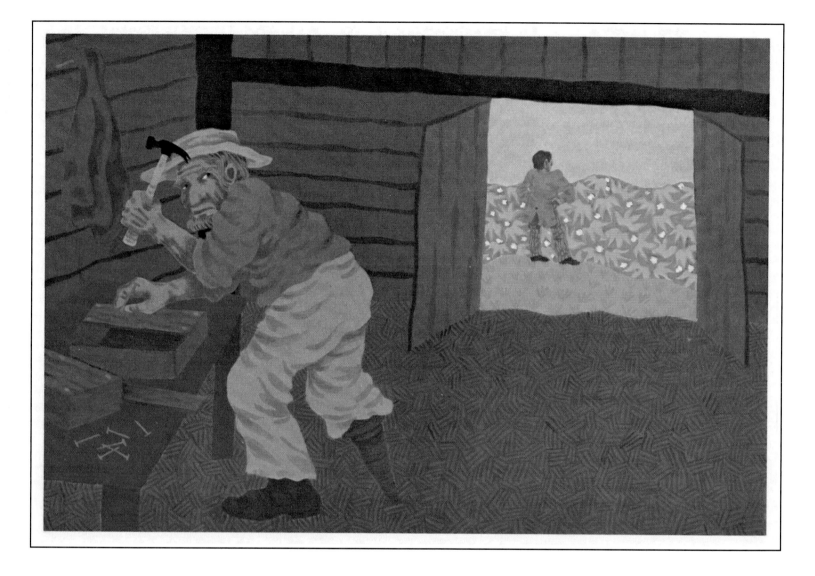

Joe had a plan.
He'd use hammer and nail and saw
and work for the master, the man
who owned the slaves
on the cotton plantation.

Joe had a plan.
At night when work was done,
he'd teach the slaves a song
that secretly told the way
to freedom.
Just follow the drinking gourd, it said.

When the song was learned
and sung all day,
Peg Leg Joe would slip away
to work for another master
and teach the song again.

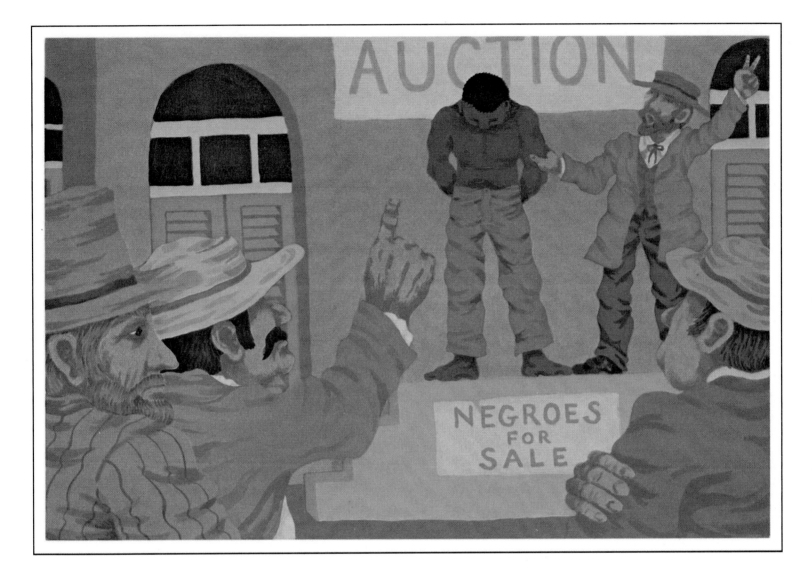

One day
a slave called Molly saw her man James
sold to another master.
James would be taken away,
their family torn apart.
Just one more night together.

A quail called in the trees that night.
Molly and James remembered Joe's song.
They sang it low.

> *When the sun comes back, and the first quail calls,*
> *Follow the drinking gourd.*
> *For the old man is a-waiting for to carry you to freedom*
> *If you follow the drinking gourd.*

They looked to the sky and saw the stars.

Taking their little son Isaiah,
old Hattie, and her grandson George,
Molly and James set out for freedom
that very night,
following the stars of the drinking gourd.
They ran all night through the fields,
till they crossed the stream to the woods.

When daylight came, they hid in the trees,
watching,
listening
for the master's hounds
set loose to find them.

But the dogs lost the runaways' scent
at the stream,
and Molly and James and Isaiah,
old Hattie and young George,
were not found.
They hid all day in the woods.

At night they walked again,
singing Joe's song
and looking for the signs
that marked the trail.

The riverbank makes a very good road,
The dead trees will show you the way.
Left foot, peg foot, traveling on,
Follow the drinking gourd.

Walking by night, sleeping by day,
for weeks they traveled on.
Sometimes berries to pick
and corn to snatch,
sometimes fish to catch,
sometimes empty bellies to sleep on.
Sometimes no stars to guide the way.

They never knew what lay ahead.
There was danger from men
who would send them back,
and danger from hungry beasts.
But sometimes a kind deed was done.

One day as they hid in a thicket
a boy from a farm found them.
In a bag of feed for the hogs in the wood
he brought bacon and corn bread to share.

Singing low, they traveled on.

> *The river ends between two hills,*
> *Follow the drinking gourd.*
> *There's another river on the other side,*
> *Follow the drinking gourd.*

On and on they followed the trail
to the river's end.
From the top of the hill they saw the new path,
another river beneath the stars
to lead them to freedom land.

The drinking gourd led them on.
The song was almost done.

> *When the great big river meets the little river,*
> *Follow the drinking gourd.*
> *For the old man is a-waiting for to carry you to freedom*
> *If you follow the drinking gourd.*

Then they climbed the last hill.
Down below was Peg Leg Joe
waiting at the wide Ohio River
to carry them across.
Their spirits rose when they saw the old man.
Molly and James and Isaiah, old Hattie and George,
ran to the shore.

Under a starry sky
Joe rowed them across the wide Ohio River.
He told them of hiding places
where they would be safe.
A path of houses stretched like a train
on a secret track leading north to Canada.
He called it the Underground Railroad.
It carried riders to freedom.

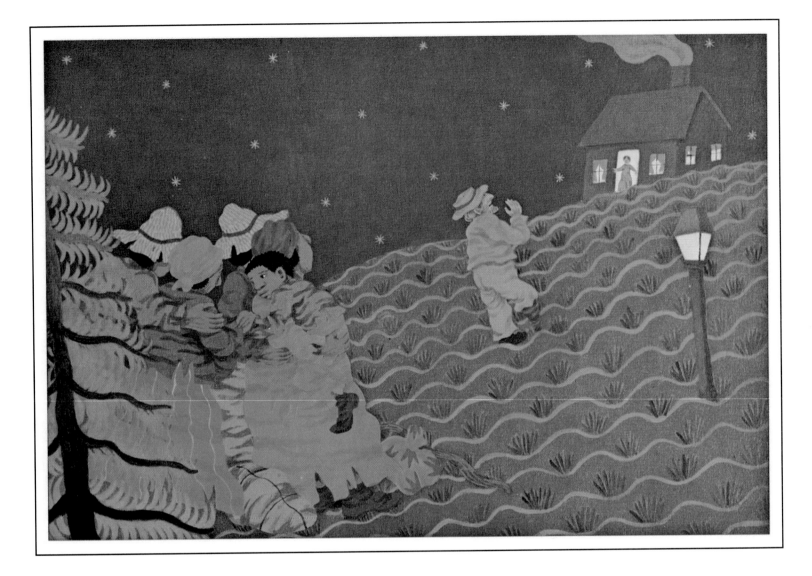

The first safe house stood on the hill.

The lamp was lit,

which meant it was safe to come.

Ragged and weary, they waited

while Joe signaled low, with a hoot like an owl.

Then the door opened wide

to welcome the freedom travelers.

They were rushed through the house
to the barn,
for the farmers knew
there were slave catchers near.
A trapdoor in the floor
took them under the barn,
to hide till it was safe to move on.
Then Peg Leg Joe went back to the river
to meet others who followed the drinking gourd.

With danger still near, too close for ease,
the farmer sent the five travelers on.
He drew a map that showed the way north
on the midnight road
to the next safe house, just over two hills.

This time James called the signal,
a hoot like an owl,
that opened the door to a Quaker farm.
The travelers were led to a secret room
hidden behind shelves.

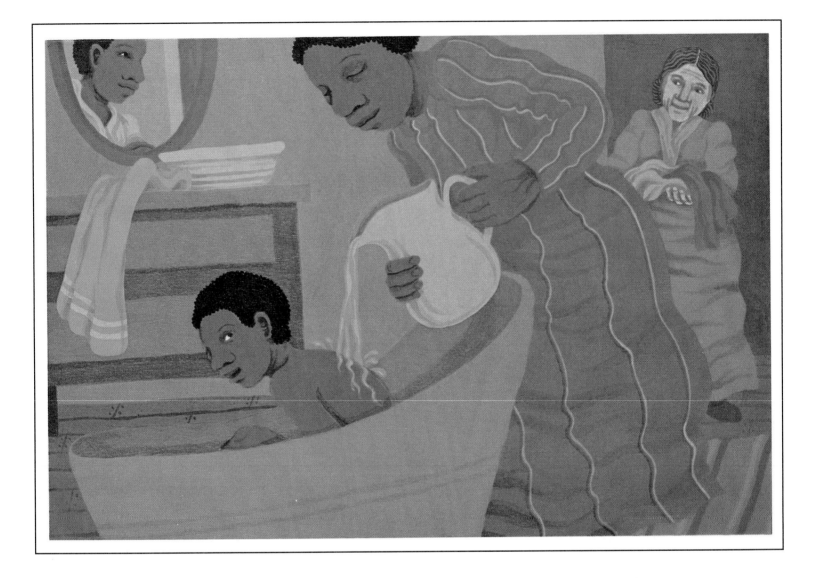

They rested here for many days
and healed their wounds.
Soft beds, full meals, new clothes, hot baths,
washed away some fear and pain.
Isaiah smiled.

When they were strong, they traveled again
from house to house on the underground trail,
still following the drinking gourd north.
Sometimes they traveled on foot,
sometimes by cart.
The wagon they rode near their journey's end
carried fruit to market
and the runaways to freedom.

At last they came to the shores of Lake Erie.
Molly and James and Isaiah,
old Hattie and young George,
climbed aboard the steamship
that would carry them across
to Canada, to freedom.
"Five more souls are safe!"
old Hattie cried.
The sun shone bright when they stepped on land.

They had followed the drinking gourd.

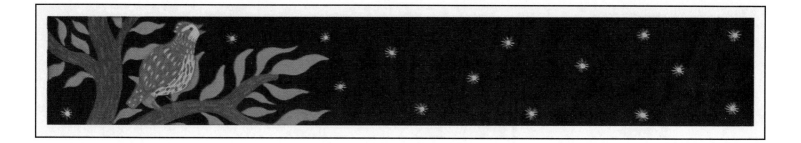

CHORUS

Fol - low _____ the drink - ing gourd! Fol - low _____ the

drink - ing gourd. _ For the old man is a - wait - ing for to

VERSE

car - ry you to free - dom If you fol - low the drink - ing gourd. When the

sun comes back, and the first quail calls, _ Fol - low _____ the

drink - ing gourd. _ For the old man is a - wait - ing for to

car - ry you to free - dom If you fol - low the drink - ing gourd.

The Underground Railroad

by Glennette Turner
illustrated by Jerry Pinkney

Long ago, African people were brought to this country as slaves. Many Americans believed that slavery was wrong. Some worked secretly to help slaves escape.

This was happening at a time when railroads were being built all over the country. So the people helping the slaves used railroad words as code words. They called the secret escape paths the Underground Railroad. The escaping slaves were called passengers. The brave people who helped them were called conductors.

Harriet Tubman was a slave who escaped from Maryland and went north. She made 19 trips back into the slave states to rescue her family and many other people. She became one of the most famous conductors on the Underground Railroad.

PACIFIC OCEAN

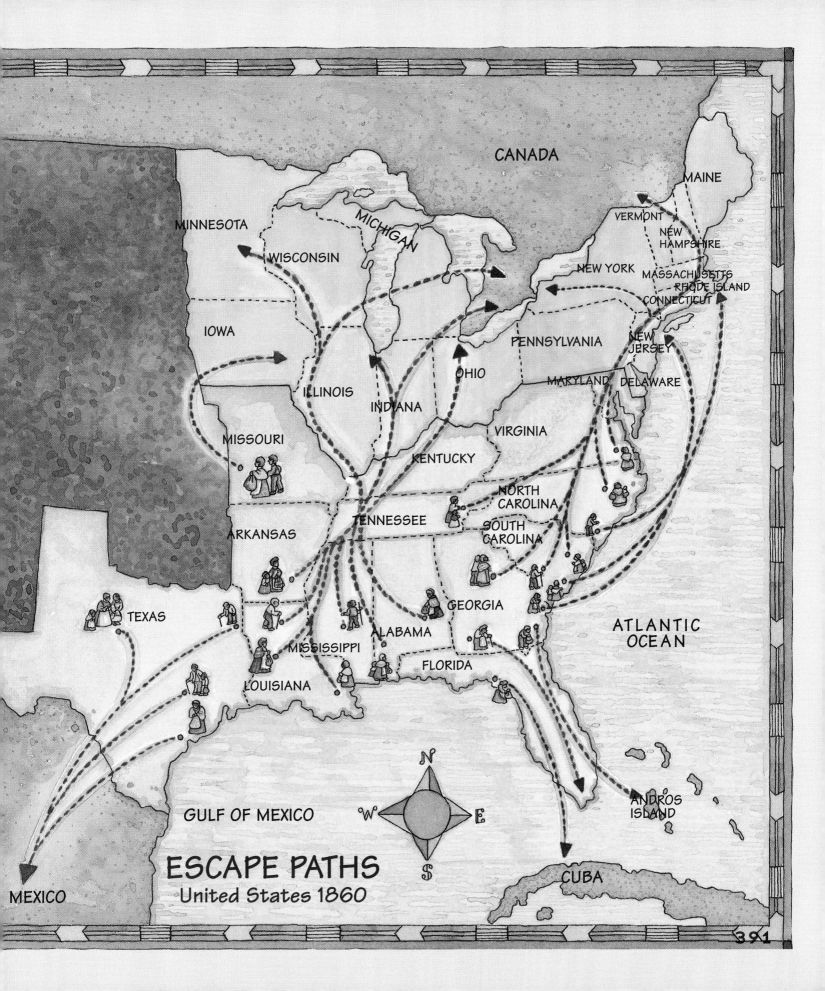

CANADA

MAINE

VERMONT

NEW HAMPSHIRE

MINNESOTA

MICHIGAN

WISCONSIN

NEW YORK

MASSACHUSETTS

RHODE ISLAND

CONNECTICUT

IOWA

PENNSYLVANIA

NEW JERSEY

OHIO

ILLINOIS

INDIANA

MARYLAND

DELAWARE

VIRGINIA

MISSOURI

KENTUCKY

NORTH CAROLINA

TENNESSEE

SOUTH CAROLINA

ARKANSAS

TEXAS

ALABAMA

GEORGIA

MISSISSIPPI

LOUISIANA

FLORIDA

ATLANTIC OCEAN

ANDROS ISLAND

GULF OF MEXICO

N

W   E

S

MEXICO

CUBA

ESCAPE PATHS
United States 1860

THINK ABOUT READING

Think about *Follow the Drinking Gourd*. Answer each question in the story map. Do your work on another sheet of paper.

Setting

1. When does this story take place?

Characters

2. Which story characters followed the drinking gourd?

Problem

3. Why did they want to go north?

4. What dangers did they face as they traveled north?

Ending

5. How did the stars help them find their way?

6. Where did they arrive at the end of their long trip?

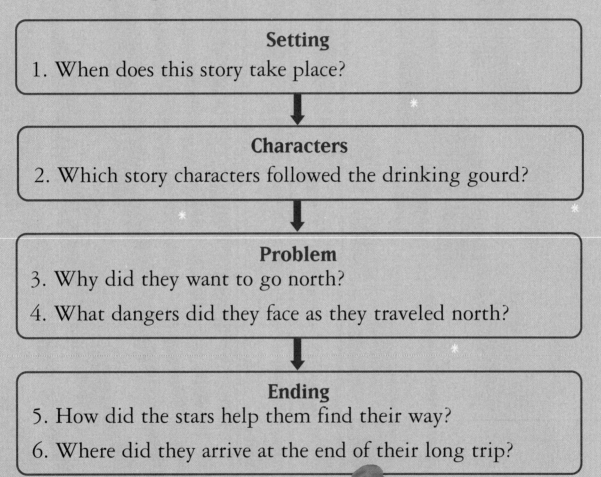

392

WRITE A JOURNAL ENTRY

Many years after she and her family finally reached Canada, Molly wrote about her journey to freedom. Write what Molly might have written in her journal.

LITERATURE CIRCLE

How does "The Underground Railroad" help you understand *Follow the Drinking Gourd*? Which path of the Underground Railroad do you think Molly, James, Isaiah, Hattie, and George followed? Why do you think there were so many different paths on the Underground Railroad?

AUTHOR
Jeanette Winter

Jeanette Winter enjoys sharing facts and feelings with children. That's why she writes and illustrates books for young readers. Many of her books tell about events that really happened. When Winter draws the pictures for her books, she tries to remember the kinds of pictures she liked when she was a young girl.

More Books by Jeanette Winter

- *Josefina*
- *Cowboy Charlie: The Story of Charles M. Russell*
- *My Name Is Georgia*

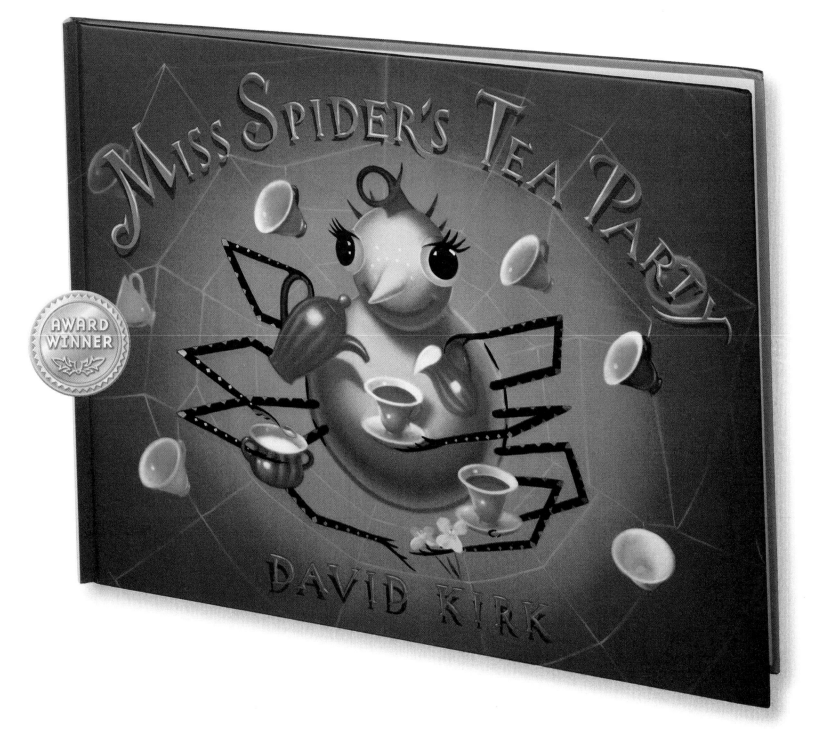

ONE lonely spider sipped her tea
While gazing at the sky.
She watched the insects on the leaves
And many flying by.
"If I had friends like these," she sighed,
"Who'd stay a while with me,
I'd sit them down on silken chairs
And serve them cakes and tea."

Two timid beetles — Ike and May —
Crept from the woodwork that same day.
But when Miss Spider begged, "Please stay?"
They shrieked, "Oh no!" and dashed away.

397

Three fireflies flew inside that night,
Their spirits high, their tails alight.
They spied the web and squeaked in fear,
"We'd better get away from here!"
The little trio did not feel
They'd care to be a spider's meal.

Four bumblebees buzzed by outside.
"Please come to tea!" Miss Spider cried.
The four ignored her swaying there.
She waved a tea towel in the air.
She took a cup and tapped the glass.
Then one bee spoke to her at last:
"We would be fools to take our tea
With anyone so spidery."

Within the shadows of the room,
Just peeking from behind a broom,
Five grinning faces bobbed and peered.
Miss Spider smiled. Her heart was cheered.
Descending for a closer look,
She danced into the gloomy nook
But sadly found those jolly mugs
Belonged, alas! to rubber bugs.

Some ants strode in, they numbered six,
But ants with spiders will not mix.
She brewed them tea from hips of roses;
The proud platoon turned up their noses.

A fine bouquet concealed its prize
Of seven dainty butterflies.
Miss Spider, watching from the wall,
Was not aware of them at all.

407

The tea table was set for eight
With saucers, cups, and silver plate.
The cakes were fresh, the service gleamed,
Yet no one would arrive, it seemed.
Her company in no demand
Left her a cup for every hand.

410

Nine spotted moths kept safe and warm
In shelter from a thunderstorm.
They stood beneath an open sash
And watched the jagged lightning flash.
Miss Spider dropped down on a thread,
A silver tray above her head.
She'd hoped to please them, but instead . . .

They flew away in mortal dread!

"They've left me all alone," she cried.
She dabbed her eyes and sadly sighed.
"It's plain no bug will ever stay."
Her tears splashed down upon the tray.

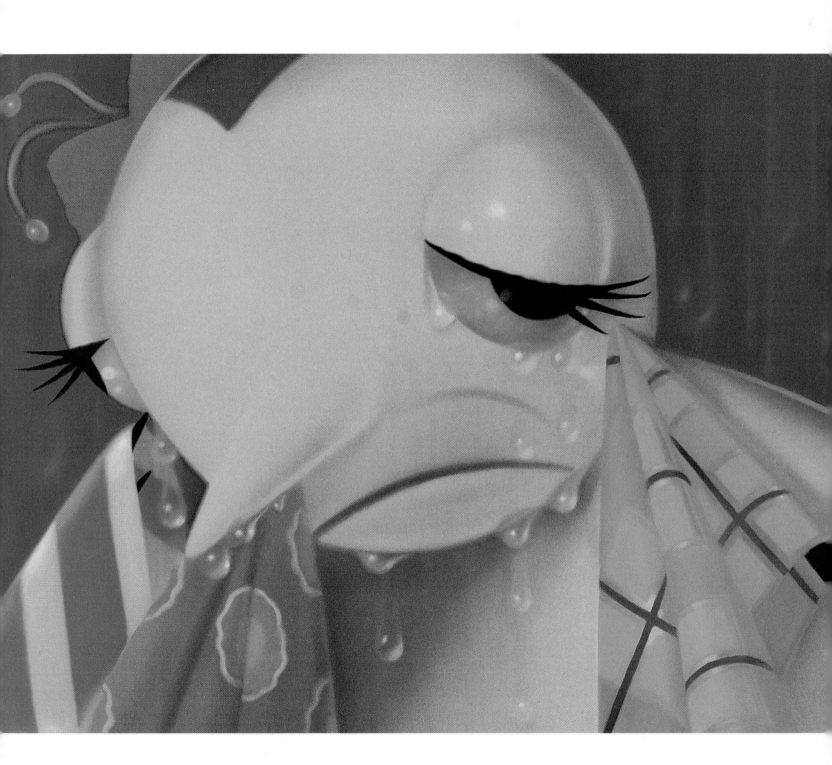

Ten tiny steaming cups of tea
Were perched atop her trembling knee.
She sipped and sobbed, then heard a cough
And turned to see a small wet moth —
A fragile thing so soaked by rain,
His wings too damp to fly again.

She smiled and took a checkered cloth
To cloak the frail and thankful moth.
They talked and snacked on tea and pie
Until his tiny wings were dry.
Then lifting him with tender care
She tossed him gently in the air.

The moth told Ike, then Ike told May,
Who went from bug to bug to say,
"There is no reason for alarm.
She's never meant us any harm!"
So later on that afternoon,
Assembled in the dining room,
Eleven insects came to tea
To share Miss Spider's courtesy.

Twelve tender violets in a vase
Presented at Miss Spider's place
Set by her chair, so neatly spun.
She munched the blossoms, one by one.
Her friends were glad to watch her feast
Upon the floral centerpiece.
It was a great relief to see
She ate just flowers and drank just tea.
Miss Spider's reputation grew.
Before too long our hostess knew
Each bug who crawled or hopped or flew
And all their lovely children too.

THINK ABOUT READING

1. What kind of insect are Ike and May?

2. Why won't the insects stay for tea with Miss Spider?

3. Why do you think the butterflies stay hidden and don't say anything to Miss Spider?

4. Look at the last picture of Miss Spider. What does the picture tell us about how she feels?

5. What might have happened if the little moth had not gotten too wet to fly?

WRITE AN INVITATION

For her next tea party, Miss Spider wants to send written invitations. Write an invitation she could send. Add some pictures or other decorations to the invitation.

LITERATURE CIRCLE

Maybe Miss Spider should have tried a different way of making friends. What do you think she could have done? Talk about your ideas.

AUTHOR
DAVID KIRK

David Kirk really likes spiders and insects—but he doesn't keep them as pets. He has several other kinds of pets. Kirk has two dogs named Emma and Polly and a hamster named Gabby. He also has two goldfish.

Kirk grew up in Ohio, where he learned about insects and painting. Today, among his other projects, he writes poems about bugs.

MORE BOOKS BY DAVID KIRK

- *Miss Spider's Wedding*
- *Miss Spider's New Car*
- *Miss Spider's ABC*

You will find all your vocabulary words in ABC order in the Glossary. This page shows you how to use it.

This is the **word** you look up. It is the **entry word**.

volcano

an opening in the ground from which hot melted rocks and steam come

*That **volcano** looks like a mountain with a big hole in the top.*

Look here to find the **meaning** of the word.

A **sentence** helps you know how the word can be used.

A **picture** or **photograph** helps you know what the entry word means.

426

amazing

surprising

*The huge pile of snow on our street is **amazing**.*

auditions

tryouts for a part in a show

*Nyoka sang three songs at the **auditions**.*

ballet

a kind of dance

*John and Maria went to see a **ballet**.*

ballet

batter

a liquid mix of eggs, sugar, and flour that is baked into cakes or cookies

*Pour the **batter** into a cake pan.*

bitter

sharp, stinging

*The **bitter** wind stings our faces.*

blew

moved by air

*When I **blew** my whistle, it made a loud sound.*

blowhole

the breathing hole of a whale on top of its head

*A whale blows air out of its **blowhole**.*

bouquet

a bunch of picked or cut flowers

*Sarah had red roses in her **bouquet**.*

brook

a small stream

*Fish swim in the **brook**.*

427

calves

young whales

*We saw a mother whale swimming with her **calves**.*

charcoal

a dark material made by burning wood

*The artist drew a picture with **charcoal**.*

charming

nice to be with

*Our new neighbor is a **charming** woman.*

cheered

shouted encouragement or approval

*My friends **cheered** loudly when I won the race.*

chirped

made the short, sharp, high sound that a bird makes

*The birds **chirped** noisily at sunrise.*

comfortable

giving a nice feeling

*The pillow was a **comfortable** place to rest his head.*

company

companionship

*I enjoy the **company** of my friends.*

considerate

kind, thoughtful of others' feelings

*It is **considerate** to ask a new classmate to play with you at recess.*

country

a land that people live in

*The United States is a **country** in North America.*

cozy

comfortable and warm

*The fire in the big fireplace made us feel **cozy**.*

crayons

sticks of colored wax used for writing or drawing

*He drew that picture with **crayons**.*

crayons

cried

shouted out loudly

*As it started to rain, Dad
cried, "Run!"*

crooned

sung or murmured in a soft voice

*The baby fell asleep as her mother
crooned her favorite song.*

crumb

a tiny piece of bread or cake

The bird ate every crumb I dropped.

disaster

an event that causes much trouble
or pain

*The storm was a disaster that blew
out many windows.*

dive

to go into the water
with your head first

*I close my eyes when
I dive into the water.*

doorstop

something that holds a door open

*The doorstop kept the door from
slamming shut.*

dough

a thick mix of flour, eggs, and
sugar that is baked into cookies and
other foods

*We cut the cookie dough into
little stars.*

drifts

piles of snow

The drifts of snow covered the cars.

erupting

breaking open suddenly

*An erupting volcano blew steam
and lava into the air.*

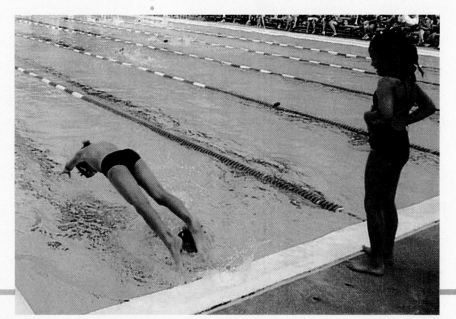

dive

equipment

the things a person needs to do a job

A fire fighter needs **equipment** *such as hoses and ladders.*

feast

to eat a fancy meal on a special occasion

We'll **feast** *on turkey for Thanksgiving.*

flashlight

a light that is small enough to carry in your hand

We used a **flashlight** *to find our way home in the dark.*

flashlight

free

not held back or kept in by anyone else

The people in America wanted to be **free** *and rule themselves.*

freedom

being able to move or act without being held back

People who live in America have **freedom** *of speech.*

frozen

turned into ice

Children skate on the **frozen** *lake.*

gasped

spoke while out of breath

"Give me water," **gasped** *the tired runner.*

gear

the tools and other things a person needs to do a job or an activity

We left the tents and other camping **gear** *under the big tree.*

glaze

a thin sugar icing

A doughnut with **glaze** *tastes extra sweet.*

grumpy

in a bad mood

Some people are **grumpy** *early in the morning.*

helmet

a hard hat that protects the head

*Ian fell off his bike, but his **helmet** protected his head.*

hissed

made a "ssss" noise like a snake to show you didn't like something

*"Quiet" **hissed** the crowd when Jordan talked during the movie.*

hoot

to make a noise like an owl

*Kimiko can **hoot** just like an owl.*

horrid

very bad, terrible

*The storm made a **horrid** mess in the park.*

hostess

a woman who has a party or entertains guests

*Grandma was the **hostess** at the party.*

hounds

hunting dogs

*The **hounds** ran through the woods.*

howl

to make a noise like the cry of a wolf

*We heard the dog **howl** when he hurt his paw.*

howling

a noise like the cry of a wolf

*The **howling** of the wind kept us awake.*

humpback

a black-and-white whale with a humplike fin

*The **humpback** whale's hump is made of fat.*

hungry

wanting food

*Jared was very **hungry** after playing all day.*

hound

431

hydrant

hydrants

water pipes that stick out of the street and are used for fighting fires

*The fire fighters got water from the **hydrants** to fight the fire.*

imaginary

make-believe, not real

*The talking animals in the story are **imaginary**.*

independence

freedom to rule yourself

*America won its **independence** from England.*

journey

a trip

*We rode the bus on our **journey** to the beach.*

jungle

land in warm tropical areas that is covered with trees and vines

*Monkeys swing from vines in the **jungle**.*

kind

nice, helpful to others

*The boy was **kind** to his little brother.*

lava

hot, melted rock that comes out of a volcano

***Lava** is flowing down the sides of the volcano.*

lava

meadow

a field of grass, often where animals graze

*Sheep were standing in the **meadow**.*

medium-sized

of a size between small and large
*The **medium-sized** shirt fit better
than the small one.*

mixed

stirred different things together
*Dad **mixed** lettuce and tomatoes to
make salad.*

mobile

a kind of sculpture that hangs from
the ceiling and moves
*The glass birds in the **mobile** seemed
to fly.*

mountainside

the side of a very high piece of land
*Cory hiked up the **mountainside**.*

munched

chewed with a crunching sound
*Jake **munched** popcorn during
the movie.*

oven

the inside of a stove, where food
is baked
*Bake the cake in the **oven**.*

paint

to make a picture with paints
*I am going to **paint** a picture
of my little brother.*

paintbrushes

brushes used to paint a picture or
cover something with paint
*The artist used many **paintbrushes**
to paint the picture.*

painting

a picture made by using paints
*The artist hung her **painting** on
the wall.*

painting

patch

a small piece of ground, or a small part of something

*There is a **patch** of beans in our garden.*

patterns

repeating arrangements of shapes and figures

*Bright **patterns** were painted on the walls of the baby's room.*

pictures

things you draw, paint, or take with a camera

*I like to draw **pictures** of people at the beach.*

pitch

to move suddenly from being flat to being crooked or at an angle

*The earthquake made the floor **pitch** and shake.*

rolled

made something flat by pushing a rounded object over it

*Grandpa **rolled** out the cookie dough.*

scent

a smell

*The **scent** of the flowers is wonderful.*

scolded

told someone that something is wrong in an angry way

*Mom **scolded** me for not doing my homework.*

scream

a loud, scared cry

*You might **scream** when you watch a scary movie.*

sculpture

a work of art carved or shaped out of a solid material such as stone

*We went to see the **sculpture** at the museum.*

sculpture

434

secretly

done in a hidden way

*I **secretly** put the note in his pocket.*

shapes

the forms or outlines of objects

*A circle and a square are two different **shapes**.*

shouts

loud calls

*Eric **shouts** when he is happy.*

shrieked

gave a sudden, loud, sharp cry

*I **shrieked** when I saw the snake.*

sighed

let out a long, deep breath because of sadness, tiredness, or relief

*"Will I ever get home?" **sighed** the lost girl.*

sipped

drank slowly in small amounts

*Pedro **sipped** his cocoa because it was hot.*

skidded

slid sideways

*The car **skidded** on the icy road.*

spout

a stream of water

*You can see the whale's **spout** when it blows air out of its blowhole.*

squeaked

made a short, high sound like the noise of a mouse

*The mouse **squeaked** as it ran away.*

stunning

very beautiful

*The queen's costume was **stunning**.*

style

the way in which something is made or done

*Using bright colors can be part of an artist's **style**.*

sugar

a sweet substance used in food and drinks

*Rashawna puts milk and **sugar** on her cereal.*

sweet

nice, easy to like

*The story is about a **sweet** girl.*

swirling

moving around in circles

*The leaves were **swirling** in the wind.*

tea

a drink made from dried leaves

*My aunt drinks hot **tea** with her breakfast.*

texture

the feel of something, especially its roughness or smoothness

*A kitten's fur has a smooth **texture**.*

theater

a place to see movies or plays

*The **theater** was showing a good movie.*

town

a place with houses, stores, and schools or a small group of houses that makes up a community

*The library is in the center of **town**.*

tray

a flat container for carrying or serving things

*Max dropped his lunch **tray**.*

uniforms

special clothes worn by people doing different jobs

*The **uniforms** of our police officers are tan.*

uniform

village

a small group of houses that make up a community

*Luke and Dana live in the same **village**.*

vivid

bright

*Jorge used **vivid** colors in his painting.*

volcano

an opening in the ground from which hot melted rocks and steam can come

*That **volcano** looks like a mountain with a big hole in the top.*

walkie-talkies

radio sets that are carried and used by people to talk to each other

*The forest workers carry **walkie-talkies** on the trail.*

war

a fight between groups of people

*The **war** went on for three years.*

whales

very large animals that live in the ocean

***Whales** are some of the biggest animals alive.*

wicked

very, very bad

*The **wicked** character in the tale finally learned his lesson.*

yard

an area of ground next to a house, or an enclosed area used for a special purpose

*The bunnies live in the **yard** behind my house.*

whales

Acknowledgments

Grateful acknowledgment is made to the following sources for permission to reprint from previously published material. The publisher has made diligent efforts to trace the ownership of all copyrighted material in this volume and believes that all necessary permissions have been secured. If any errors or omissions have inadvertently been made, proper corrections will gladly be made in future editions.

Cover, Title Page, and Unit 6 *Lend a Hand* Table of Contents: From MISS SPIDER'S TEA PARTY by David Kirk. Copyright © 1994 by Callaway & Kirk Company. Reprinted by permission of Scholastic Press, a division of Scholastic Inc., in association with Callaway & Kirk Company. Miss Spider, and all related characters, are trademarks of Callaway & Kirk Company.

Unit 4 *Story Studio* Table of Contents: From AMAZING GRACE by Mary Hoffman, illustrated by Caroline Binch. Illustrations copyright © 1991 by Caroline Binch. Used by permission of Dial Books for Young Readers, a division of Penguin Putnam Inc.

Unit 5 *Animal World* Table of Contents: From "Balto, The Dog Who Saved Nome" from FIVE TRUE DOG STORIES by Margaret Davidson. Illustrations for this version by Cathie Bleck. Illustrations copyright © 1996 by Scholastic Inc. Published by Scholastic Inc.

Unit 4 *Story Studio*:
Unit Opener: From LITTLE GRUNT & THE BIG EGG by Tomie dePaola. Copyright © 1990 by Tomie dePaola. All rights reserved. Reprinted by permission of Holiday House, Inc.

"The Gingerbread Man" from THE GINGERBREAD MAN retold by Jim Aylesworth, illustrated by Barbara McClintock. Text copyright © 1998 by Jim Aylesworth. Illustrations copyright © 1998 by Barbara McClintock. Reprinted by permission of Scholastic Inc.

"Tricksters from Around the World" from *Storyworks*® magazine, October 1997, Vol. 5, No. 2, pages 24–25. Copyright © 1997 by Scholastic Inc. Reprinted by permission of Scholastic Inc.

"Abuelo and the Three Bears" from ABUELO AND THE THREE BEARS by Jerry Tello, illustrated by Ana López Escrivá. Copyright © 1996 by Scholastic Inc.

Selection from "Who's Been Sleeping in My Porridge?" by Colin McNaughton and illustration of the "Backyard Players." Copyright © 1990 by Colin McNaughton.

Reprinted by permission of Ideals Children's Books, an imprint of Hambleton-Hill Publishing, Inc., Nashville, TN. All rights reserved. Also by permission of Walker Books Limited.

"Little Grunt & the Big Egg" from LITTLE GRUNT AND THE BIG EGG by Tomie dePaola. Copyright © 1990 by Tomie dePaola. All rights reserved. Reprinted by permission of Holiday House, Inc.

"Red Riding Hood" from RED RIDING HOOD by James Marshall. Copyright © 1987 by James Marshall. Used by permission of Dial Books for Young Readers, a division of Penguin Putnam Inc.

"And Still More Tales": Cover from RED RIDING HOOD by Beatrice Schenk de Regniers, illustrated by Edward Gorey. Illustration copyright © 1972 by Edward Gorey. Reprinted by permission of Atheneum Books for Young Readers, Simon & Schuster Children's Publishing Division. Cover and detail from the book cover from RUBY by Michael Emberley. Copyright © 1990 by Michael Emberley. Reprinted by permission of Little, Brown and Company. Cover from FLOSSIE THE FOX by Patricia C. McKissack, pictures by Rachel Isadora. Pictures copyright © 1986 by Rachel Isadora. Used by permission of Dial Books for Young Readers, a division of Penguin Putnam Inc. Cover from THE PRINCESS AND THE FROG by Rachel Isadora. Copyright © 1989 by Rachel Isadora. Reprinted by permission of Greenwillow Books, a division of William Morrow & Company, Inc. Cover from THE FROG PRINCE by Edith H. Tarcov, illustrated by James Marshall. Illustration copyright © 1974 by James Marshall. Reprinted by permission of Scholastic Inc. Cover from THE FROG PRINCE CONTINUED by Jon Scieszka, illustrated by Steve Johnson. Illustration copyright © 1991 by Steve Johnson. Used by permission of Viking Penguin, a division of Penguin Putnam Inc. Cover from CINDERELLA: THE UNTOLD STORY as told by Russell Shorto, illustrated by T. Lewis. Illustration copyright © 1990 by T. Lewis. Reprinted by permission of Carol Publishing Group. A Birch Lane Press Book. Cover and detail from the book cover from SIDNEY RELLA AND THE GLASS SNEAKER by Bernice Myers. Copyright © 1985 by Bernice Myers. Reprinted by arrangement with Simon & Schuster Books for Young Readers, Simon and Schuster Children's Publishing Division. Cover from YEH-SHEN: A CINDERELLA STORY FROM CHINA by Ai-Ling Louie, illustrated by Ed Young. Illustration copyright © 1982

by Ed Young. Reprinted by permission of Philomel Books. Cover from JACK AND THE BEANSTALK, illustrated by Matt Faulkner. Illustrations copyright © 1986 by Matt Faulkner. Reprinted by permission of Scholastic Inc. Cover from JACK AND THE BEANSTALK by Alan Garner, illustrated by Julek Heller. Illustration copyright © 1992 by Julek Heller. Used with permission of Dell Books, a division of Bantam Doubleday Dell Publishing Group, Inc. Cover from JIM AND THE BEANSTALK by Raymond Briggs. Illustration copyright © 1970 by Raymond Briggs. Reprinted by permission of Coward-McCann, Inc. Cover from THE MOUSE BRIDE: A MAYAN FOLK TALE by Judith Dupré, illustrated by Fabricio Vanden Broeck. Illustration copyright © 1993 by Fabricio Vanden Broeck. Reprinted by permission of Alfred A. Knopf, Inc., a division of Random House, Inc. Cover from MOUSE'S MARRIAGE by Anne Bower Ingram, illustrated by Junko Morimoto. Illustration copyright © 1985 by Junko Morimoto. Used by permission of Penguin Putnam Inc. Cover and detail from the book cover from THE MOUSE BRIDE: A CHINESE FOLKTALE, retold by Monica Chang, illustrated by Lesley Liu. Copyright © 1992 by Yuan-Liou Publishing Co., Ltd. Reprinted by permission.

"Amazing Grace" from AMAZING GRACE by Mary Hoffman, illustrated by Caroline Binch. Text copyright © 1991 by Mary Hoffman. Illustrations copyright © 1991 by Caroline Binch. Used by permission of Dial Books for Young Readers, a division of Penguin Putnam Inc.

"An Amazing Peter Pan" from PETER PAN. Theatre program and cast list is used by kind permission of The People's Light & Theatre Company.

Unit 5 *Animal World*: "Stellaluna" from STELLALUNA by Janell Cannon. Copyright © 1993 by Janell Cannon. Reprinted by permission of Harcourt Brace & Company.

"Balto, The Dog Who Saved Nome" from FIVE TRUE DOG STORIES by Margaret Davidson, illustrations by Cathie Bleck. Text copyright © 1977 by Margaret Davidson. Illustrations copyright © 1996 by Scholastic Inc. Published by Scholastic Inc.

Text of "Puppygarten Star" from the September 1994 issue of KID CITY MAGAZINE. Copyright © 1994 by Children's Television Workshop, New York, NY. All rights reserved. Photographs from the book ROSIE: A VISITING DOG'S STORY by Stephanie Calmenson. Photographs © 1994 by Justin Sutcliffe. Reprinted by permission of Clarion Books/Houghton Mifflin Co. All rights reserved.

"Ibis: A True Whale Story" from IBIS: A TRUE WHALE STORY by John Himmelman. Copyright © 1990 by John Himmelman. Reprinted by permission of Scholastic Inc.

"When the Monkeys Came Back" from WHEN THE MONKEYS CAME BACK. Text copyright © 1994 by Kristine L. Franklin. Illustrations copyright © 1994 by Robert Roth. Reprinted with permission of Atheneum Books for Young Readers, Simon & Schuster Children's Publishing Division.

Text from "How Artists See Animals" from HOW ARTISTS SEE ANIMALS by Colleen Carroll. Text copyright © 1996 by Colleen Carroll. Compilation, including selection of text and images, copyright © 1996 Abbeville Press. Reprinted by permission of Abbeville Press, a division of Abbeville Publishing Group.

"Animal Messengers" from COLORÍN COLORADO: THE ART OF INDIAN CHILDREN, MEXICO by the Trust for the Health of the Indian Children of Mexico. Copyright © 1993, 1994 by the Trust for the Health of the Indian Children of Mexico. Reprinted by permission of the Trust for the Health of the Indian Children of Mexico.

Unit 6 Lend a Hand: "The Little Painter of Sabana Grande" from THE LITTLE PAINTER OF SABANA GRANDE. Text copyright © 1993 by Patricia Maloney Markun. Illustrations copyright © 1993 by Robert Casilla. Reprinted by permission of Simon & Schuster Books for Young Readers, Simon & Schuster Children's Publishing Division. All rights reserved.

"My Painted House" from MY PAINTED HOUSE, MY FRIENDLY CHICKEN AND ME. Text copyright © 1994 by Maya Angelou. Illustrations copyright © 1994 by Margaret Courtney-Clarke. Reprinted by permission of Clarkson N. Potter, a division of Crown Publishers.

"Firefighters" from FIREFIGHTERS by Robert Maass. Copyright © 1989 by Robert Maass. Used by permission of Scholastic Inc.

"The Many Lives of Ben Franklin" from THE MANY LIVES OF BEN FRANKLIN by Aliki. Copyright © 1977, 1988 by Aliki Brandenburg. Reprinted by permission of Simon & Schuster Books for Young Readers, an imprint of Simon & Schuster Children's Publishing Division.

"Follow the Drinking Gourd" from FOLLOW THE DRINKING GOURD by Jeanette Winter. Copyright © 1988 by Jeanette Winter. Reprinted by arrangement with Alfred A. Knopf, Inc., a division of Random House, Inc.

Harriet Tubman illustration by Jerry Pinkney in "The Underground Railroad" from SEA TO SHINING SEA compiled by Amy L. Cohn. Illustration copyright © 1993 by Jerry Pinkney. Published by Scholastic Inc. Used by permission.

"Miss Spider's Tea Party" from MISS SPIDER'S TEA PARTY by David Kirk. Copyright © 1994 by Callaway & Kirk Company. Reprinted by permission of Scholastic Press, a division of Scholastic Inc., in association with Callaway & Kirk Company. Miss Spider, and all related characters, are trademarks of Callaway & Kirk Company.

Photography and Illustration Credits

Photos: pp. 10–11, 88–91, Suki Coughlin for Scholastic Inc.; p. 43, Courtesy Robert Casilla; pp. 44, 62, 94, 174, 194, 214, 236, 284, 362, David Waitz for Scholastic Inc.; p. 61, Courtesy Jerry Tello; pp. 121, 145, Penguin/ Putnam USA; p. 145, Frances Lincoln LTD; p. 190ml, Bob Daemmrich for Scholastic Inc.; p. 190mr, Courtesy Angela Medearis; pp. 4, 268, 269, 279, Hirshhorn Museum and Sculpture Garden, Smithsonian Institution, Washington, DC; Gift of Joseph H. Horshhorn, 1966. Photo: Lee Stalsworth. © 1995 Artists Rights Society (ARS), New York/ ADAGP, Paris.; pp. 93ml, 258tr, 260ml, 261mr, 261c, Martin Simon for Scholastic Inc.; p. 146tl, © Luis Rosendo/FPG International; p. 146mr, © Dick Sawicki/FPG International; p. 146, © Bill Losh/FPG International; p. 147, © A. Schmidecker/FPG International; pp. 147br, 258ml, 258bl, 259mr, 260tr, 260br, 261tr, Walter P. Calahan for Scholastic Inc.; p. 191, © Bill Richmond; p. 213, Courtesy Margaret Davidson; p. 232ml, Larry Maglott for Scholastic Inc.; pp. 232mr, 232c, Center for Coastal Studies, Provincetown, PA; p. 235, Elizabeth Himmelman; p. 265, Pushkin Museum of the Fine Arts, Moscow, Russia. © 1995 Succession H. Matisse, Paris/Artists Rights Society (ARS), NY. Photo: Bridgeman Art Library, London/ Superstock; pp. 266, 267, Photo: Roy Lichtenstein © Estate of Roy Lichtenstein; p. 270, Philadelphia Museum of Art; The Louise and Walter Arensberg Collection © 1995 Artists Rights Society (ARS), New York/ VG Bild-Kunst, Bonn; p. 271, Philadelphia Museum of Art; The Louise and Walter Arensberg Collection © 1995 Artists Rights Society (ARS), New York/ VG Bild-Kunst, Bonn.

Photo: Graydon Wood; pp. 272, 273, 278bl, Van Gogh Museum, Amsterdam, The Netherlands. Photo: Art Resource/ NY; p. 275, © The Georgia O'Keefe Foundation/ Artists Roghts Society (ARS), NY. Photo: Malcolm Varon, NYC.; p. 279, Abbeville Publishing; pp. 282ml, 282c, 283br, Marcia Keegan for Scholastic Inc.; p. 283c, © John Cancalosi/DRK Photo; p. 300, Ken Karp for Scholastic Inc.; p. 345, Henry Holt & Co.; pp. 356, 358, Valerie Sokolova for Scholastic Inc.; p. 361, Harper Collins; p. 393, Courtesy Jeanette Winter; pp. 426tl, 437tr, © Soames Summerheys/Photo Researchers; p. 427br, © Bill Bachman/ Photo Researchers; p. 429bl, © Blair Seitz/ Photo Researchers; p. 430bl, Richard Megna for Scholastic Inc.; p. 432tl, © Tim Davis/Photo Researchers; p. 432br, © Richard Hutchings/ Photo Researchers; p. 433br, © Bill Losh/FPG International; p. 434br, Musee National D'art De Moderne, Paris/ Centre National D'art De Culture. Photo: Georges Pompidou/ SuperStock; p. 436br, Marcia Keegan for Scholastic Inc.; p. 437tc, © Francoise Gohier/Photo Researchers.

Cover: David Kirk

Illustrations: pp.60–61: Ana López Escrivá for Scholastic Inc.p.145: Fran Lee for Scholastic Inc. pp.194–209, 212–213: Cathie Bleck for Scholastic Inc. p.280: Steve Schudlich for Scholastic Inc. pp.282–283 b/g: Jackie Snider for Scholastic Inc. pp.356–359: Valerie Sokolova for Scholastic Inc.

Illustrated Author Photos: pp. 43, 61, 93, 121, 145, 345, 361, 389, 393: Gabe DiFiore for Scholastic Inc. pp. 191, 213, 235, 279: David Frank for Scholastic Inc.